Line of Communications

A Tour of Duty:
Turkey 1963-1965

Sondra Garner

For information about permission to reproduce selections from this book write to Permissions, MFM Publishing, 11664 National Boulevard, Suite 316, Los Angeles, California 90064 U.S.A.

MFM Publishing and the MFM Publishing logo are trademarks of MFM Publishing. www.maxfmedia.com

The Library of Congress has cataloged the paperback edition as follows: Library of Congress Control Number: 2018913168

Summary: In 1963, Sondra Garner, her three small children in tow, goes to join her husband, an Air Force Officer stationed at Incirlik, Turkey. While there her son is kidnapped and separately her husband is taken hostage by the Turkish Government to force the United States to support Turkey's invasion of Cyprus.

K-ISBN 978-1-731-15583-2 paperback

Published in the United States by MFM Publishing, Los Angeles, CA U.S.A.

Editing, Book Design, Cover Design, and Cover Photography by Manuel Freedman

Interior photography courtesy and used by permission of the Author.

Manufactured in the United States of America

Dedication

To Author Lori Howell-Thompson for your love, generosity and guidance through this journey of writing.

Jesse Garner for your endurance of my time spent to write this book and your support.

Sandy Stultz and her Jet Jockey husband, Dick Stultz for their encouragement and moral support. For Dick and his artistry in bringing life and memories back, to old photos.

All of you who insisted this story had to be told, especially Paul Petersen, I appreciate, your nudging me to do so.

About the Author

As a child and teenager, Sondra and her mother traveled whenever possible to foreign countries, thus evoking Sondra's curiosity about other lands. Her Mother's 'Travel Bible' was the book, *Europe on Five Dollars a Day*.

Sondra Graduated High school, started college, was married to a Military Officer and had children at an early age.

Eight years after their marriage her husband was deployed to Turkey. There began the nightmare of his being taken hostage by the Turkish government and Sondra's determination to save his life.

After returning from her ordeal in Turkey, Sondra remained dedicated to helping the military family while serving as a local and International elected officer for both Officer and Enlisted organizations. As Vice President and Legislation Committee Chair for AFSA Auxiliary, she fought vigorously to protect the medical benefits for her fellow military families, winning the AFSA Presidential award.

After her children were grown, Sondra called upon her early experience—having grown up in a family run business—and her Degree in International marketing to develop a large International Customer Satisfaction analysis company.

Her love of nature, mountains, water and beautiful blue skies, drove her to relocate to Lake Tahoe. To this day, she is fervently proud to be part of the military family, "Proud to be an American!"

Table of Contents

This Book ~ is based on the true story of an Air Force Officer who was assigned to a tour of duty in Turkey in 1963. Moreover, it is the story of his young wife and their small children who joined him.

It tells of her heart-wrenching fight to save him from certain death at the hands of the Turkish Government. The desperation she felt and the unfaltering courage she showed while ensnared in a tug of war between two countries—two different worlds—is unimaginable! You will feel the fear of two parents when their son was kidnapped!

Turkey was at war politically with Cyprus at the time of her husband's deployment. The Turkish Government was resolute in their commitment to force the United States to support the Turkish invasion of Cyprus.

As a means to gain leverage against the United States, the Turkish Government arrested three American military men on trumped-up charges and held them as political prisoners. The Turkish Government, determined to prove they were in control, would escalate the charges according to the amount of pressure the Turkish authorities wished to assert against the United States.

Back home in the United States, there was no mention in the news media about the military men held in prison. It is clear the United States Government was committed to keeping the matter quiet at all costs.

This is a poignant story of ardent love, humor, intrigue and unmitigated fear!

A Little Personal Background

Chase

My husband, Chase, was a dedicated Air Force officer, a caring husband, and a devoted father. He was several years older than I and had been in the Air Force for six years before we met. Prior to being assigned to Turkey, Chase had served in Viet Nam, Korea, and Japan. He was honored to serve as one of NASA's Medical Rescue Team for the space program from its inception.

Chase's father was an engineer for a national development company and subsequently traveled a lot. He was out of town on a business trip when his wife went into labor. Tragically, as she was driving herself to the hospital, a drunk driver broadsided her car.

As faith would have it, a hospital intern was on his way home from work after finishing a twelve-hour shift in the emergency room. When he came upon the accident, he jumped out of his car and immediately pulled her flaccid body from her car. She struggled to speak to him as she took her last breath and died in his arms.

The intern, realizing he had no time to spare and only moments to deliver her baby, placed the woman in the back of his station wagon. Fortunately, he had his shaving kit with him! With a sense of extreme urgency, he removed a clean razor blade and delivered her baby boy by cesarean section. He carefully wrapped the baby in his coat and then rushed back to the emergency room where he had just gotten off duty.

Consequently, Chase's father, who lived in upstate New York, now had a newborn baby boy to care for. Because he traveled often, he hired a couple to look after his newborn son as well as tend to his house.

It was sad that Chase's father seemed in some way to blame his son for his mother's death. According to the housekeeper, "The father was gone as much as possible." As a result, she and her husband essentially raised the little boy.

Chase was an outgoing boy. He was such a good student that he completed high school two years ahead of schedule. He could not wait to go on to college and then begin a military career. He was extremely proud of being able to serve his country as a member of the Air Force.

Neither Chase nor I could be present at a military function with the troops marching and ol' glory flying without having tears come to our eyes and lumps in our throat.

You know that lump...the lump that comes from pride. Pride in the people who serve their country; pride and gratitude for those who have given so much; pride to be part of the military family! We were both so proud to be Americans!

Sondra

Sondra, age twenty-four, when this Turkish *adventure* began. Luckily, I already had exposure to the world beyond our U.S. borders. I had been across the pond, as they would say, and had become a seasoned Air Force wife in the eight years that Chase and I had been married.

My father died when I was twelve years old. My mother took over managing the family business. Upon the announcement of my Father's death, my Father's trusted employee absconded with much of the company's assets, which caused us to struggle financially for the first few years.

Even though we were not wealthy, my mother always found the means for us to travel. The fascination of meeting new people from other worlds and learning about their cultures and customs was ingrained in my personality. From my mother, I learned about courage, determination and curiosity. She gave me the impetus to want to learn about this earth of ours and the people walking on her soil.

In elementary school, halfway through first grade, I was moved up to second grade. One can only assume the teacher got sick of my constant chatty Cathy habit or perhaps it was because I was constantly asking her questions. I had to know the "why" of everything she taught. I will admit I was a pain in that sense. If mother told me 'no', I usually would accept her decision without a fuss but only after I knew the reason behind it. Accepting the fact something worked was not enough—I had to know the how or why.

Even though I was not Catholic, I attended a private, all-girls Catholic high school. This meant there were many motivations to aim for good grades in order to move onto college as early as possible.

No offense to the nuns but throughout the years Mother Superior and I did have a few words now and again. Actually, she talked and I listened. Then of course, I said my mandatory "Thank you, Sister" begrudgingly after each reprimand. My usual despicable offense was whispering in the chapel or talking to my best friend in class... *There is that chatty Cathy thing again.*

In my junior year, Mother Superior told my mother, "Sondra is getting bored and in order to graduate she will only have to double up on one English class." Because of her recommendation, I graduated a few months later - a few days before my 16th birthday. "She must be smart," you may be thinking...not at all. My theory is, Mother Superior simply wanted to nudge me out as soon as possible. The nuns were tough taskmasters but I loved *most* of them dearly. Through them, I received a wonderful education.

When I started college at age sixteen. I had previously spent two years of study in Switzerland and traveled through Europe with Mother in the summertime. I especially adored England, except for the weather. It seemed a natural path for my college degree to be in International Marketing with a minor in Diplomacy. I always assumed I would finish college and go to work for an embassy or some company with offices abroad.

Being a typical young person, I did not come to appreciate either my book learning or my mother's valuable lessons until later in life. There was little realization on my part that the lessons from both the nuns and my mother would come into play in such a dramatic way in the coming months and years ahead—lessons that could possibly help to save our lives!

After we were married, Chase and I were first stationed at Clark Air Force base in the Philippines. Chase left to report for duty only a couple of weeks after our wedding and I followed him a few months later. Fortunately, I was already a seasoned traveler. Suitcases, passports, and strange new customs and languages had become a part of my way of life while growing up.

Mother

Gladys, my mother, was born in Missouri and raised on a small family farm during the depression. All of her family was good hard working farmers and they instilled in her that marvelous good ol' Missouri work ethic. She had four other siblings and hated being poor and wearing hand-me-down clothes.

Mother was determined to improve her status in life, which she did in spite of the fact she only had a ninth grade formal education.

My mother had a natural talent for business and taught me, at age four, to be a little entrepreneur. I sold strawberries to customers on the block of my mother's business. Being only four years old, my clientele was limited, as I did not have permission to cross the street by myself. Luckily, my customers all knew how to make change for themselves, as I was not too swift at math at that age. My customers were most patient and I soon got the gist of making sure they gave me the correct change.

Mother and I were both convinced I, too, had a natural sales ability like her. In reality, who could resist a basket of big, ripe, homegrown strawberries, sold by a little four-year-old girl in a fluffy dress!

Mother made great sacrifices in my younger years to keep me in a private school. Although she wanted me to have the education and advantages she never had as a child, she did upon occasion resent me for having those very opportunities she never had while growing up. She was an extremely tough taskmaster, but she loved me in her own special way.

"Mom, I am truly grateful for all you gave to me. You taught me by example that I could accomplish anything I made up my mind to do."

There He Was...Beside the Road

It was Sunday and I was just backing out of our driveway in Denver, when Mother waved for me to stop. I was taking my cousin Cindy back home when Mother decided she wished to go, too. She preferred to take her Oldsmobile instead of my little Chevy convertible.

Uncle Patrick, my mother's brother, had a large cattle ranch just outside Hugo, Colorado. He had four daughters and we usually brought the youngest one to Denver for part of the summer.

It was a very hot summer day and there was no air conditioning in my Uncle's house. We spent a few hours at their place. He and mother talked while I played a few board games with my cousins. Normally my oldest cousin and I would ride horses out on the ranch when I was there, but not in that heat.

Mother and I were both eager to leave and head back home to Denver. We had a glass of ice tea, said our goodbyes and headed out.

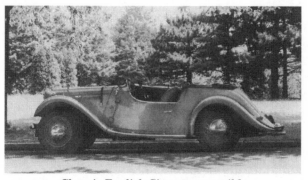

Chase's English Singer convertible.

As we were chatting about my cousin's visit, we came upon this oil-covered fellow on the side of the highway. He was standing beside a little red convertible sports car looking quite dejected. His car was an English Singer, to be exact, which looks like an old MG with a ducktail. The car's oil line had broken and it had spewed oil all over him making him look worse than a hobo!

In spite of the looks of this pathetic male, my mother stopped to see if he needed help. Ok, so I will admit we were about fifty miles from Denver, in the middle of nowhere, with only sagebrush for miles. I personally thought her brain had had a meltdown from the heat, but then she was always an easy touch for strays or those in need.

After finding out this oil soaked fella was Officer in the Air Force and that he was on his way to be stationed in the Philippines, she offered to drive him to Denver where he could find a place to get his car fixed the following day. Mother said she would make arrangements in the morning to have his car towed to Denver.

Since it was Sunday, and there were no tow trucks available, we had no alternative but to leave his car by the side of the road. He attached a note to the windshield explaining that the car was not abandoned and hoped the sheriff would not tow it away. He wrote his information, our telephone number and said that the car was to be towed to Denver the following day.

I insisted we put him in the front seat, feeling it would be safer. I figured I could knock him in the head with a book from the back seat if he gave us any trouble! We got a blanket from the trunk of mother's car, put it over the front seat for our oily passenger, and down the highway we went.

As we continued on to Denver, mother interrogated the poor man the entire time. After her thorough investigation of most of his life, from birth through the present, she offered him use of our guest room for a few days or at least until he could get his car repaired.

It appeared that this tall, oily, blob had quickly become her new best friend... *Now I knew this woman had gone completely berserk!*

The first thing he did after getting to the house was to take a shower and then report to the kitchen where mother and I were fixing dinner... *All I have to say is that he cleaned up real good and definitely got this young girl's attention!*

After dinner, mother promptly informed me I would be showing him around Denver until his car was repaired. "What a drag," I thought. I had made other plans with my friends, which did not include being a tour guide.

Then again, he was tall and good-looking and I could show him off a bit to my girlfriends...so maybe this had a plus!

We spent the next week seeing Denver and the surrounding area.

This stranger was growing on me!

One day we climbed one of the mountains just outside Denver. As we sat side-by-side soaking in the splendor of the view before us, a feeling of complete tranquility and belonging embodied both of us.

Chase leaned over, took my face in his hand, and ever so gently kissed me... From that moment on, we became one.

It so happened while we were doing the dishes the next evening we were 'busted' for smooching. The neighbors next door, a sweet older couple, let us know nicely the following day they had seen us. They did say, however, that we were a "darling couple" and they did not rat on us to mother!

In the days to follow, we talked all day and late into the night. We shared a plethora of thoughts. It was amazing how close we became in one short week and how much we had discovered about each other.

Since Mother was very strict and protective, Chase

thought it best to ask her permission to write letters to me when he left. He asked her if he could talk to her for a few minutes. She somberly said, "Come down to the rumpus room." I was certain mother would get into a snit over Chase even asking permission to write letters to me—partly because Chase was several years older than I was.

Mother was not necessarily a fan of the male gender, or so it had appeared, up until this point in my life. She had already been married four times which would somewhat account for her attitude toward men. But, she was totally impressed with Chase.

Exactly fifty-two long minutes later, they both emerged. Mother went to her bedroom, brought something out, and handed it to Chase. Then, she disappeared.

I dreaded what his response would be. I was sure she had said "no" in several languages and that I would certainly catch her wrath for him having even asked her.

Chase came over to me and said, "I think you realize I have fallen in love with you. Do you love me, too?" *This was not at all, what I had expected to hear from him—to say the least!*

The only response I could think of at that moment was, "I know I will miss you terribly when you leave."

"Sondra, would you consider marrying me?" Chase asked.

Not wanting to hurt the poor guy's feelings, I said, "Yes, probably." *When I said "yes, probably", I was thinking he meant 'someday!'*

Chase went on to say, "Your mother told me she had not married the love of her life when she was your age and had regretted it ever since. She said she knows we are meant for each other." He continued, "She gave us permission to get married...now...before I leave for the Philippines."

I faintly remember Chase slipping my mother's emerald and diamond ring onto my finger. (Emerald is my birthstone and the ring was one I had loved since I was a little girl.) The ring now became my engagement ring, I guessed!

I was more than shocked! I was totally dazed and don't remember saying "ok, yes, sure" or anything even remotely close. I was definitely, caught up in the moment!

The next morning the three of us, Mother, Chase and I, packed our small suitcases and were off to New Mexico. Since I was underage, mother had to sign permission for us to marry! Because there was no waiting time, Chase and I were married the following morning in New Mexico by a Justice of the Peace. Evidently, my two conspirators had worked out the plan to get married in New Mexico during the fifty-two long minutes in the rumpus room.

In a little white chapel in an old house on the corner, we were legally made one.

To this day, I will never quite figure out what really happened.

It was late when we finally arrived at the hotel the evening before we got married. Chase's room was on the third floor; Mother's and my room was on the second. I woke up the next morning long before dawn with a severe case of cold feet in regards to this 'getting married deal.'

I could only think, "Had my mother lost her mind?" I panicked, "What the heck am I doing here? I have not the foggiest idea what or why. How can I get out of this? Run! Get the car keys and drive home!"

What common sense I had left told me the

repercussions would be too great from mother if I left her stranded in New Mexico. I decided to scrap that idea and I lay back down to think.

Soon the thoughts of Chase—his gentle kisses, his compassion, our oneness on the mountain, calmed my entire being.

It so happened I was not the only cold-footed victim on this journey. Our brave, tough, military officer seemed to be afflicted with the same syndrome.

Chase's version and discussion with himself went like this:

I definitely had a case of cold feet. I woke up in a panic and realized if I tried to go through the hotel lobby, I was sure Sondra's mom would catch me.

My alternative was to go out the window. I realized that I was on the third floor and if I were to jump, I would break every bone in my body. My Commanding Officer would not be happy.

"Oh, hell", I thought, "What's the use? I don't have a car to go anywhere anyway. I'm screwed." I sat down in the chair to ponder my dilemma. Soon I realized that I wanted to do dishes with Sondra. I wanted to raise children with her. I was lusting after her, I will admit, but also it seemed the two of us just fit as one. I knew my life was meant to take this path.

After we returned to Denver, Chase and I repacked our clothes and then spent the next week on our honeymoon in Aspen—just the two of us on this trip.

The sequence was a wee bit out of the ordinary but when we got back, mother hosted a lovely reception for the newly married couple.

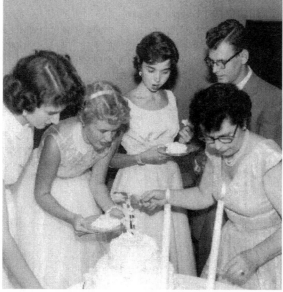

Sondra and Chase's wedding.

Chase arranged to have his little sports car transported by truck to Oakland for shipment to his next assignment: Clark Air Force Base in the Philippines.

Chase flew to Oakland with the intent of leaving in the next few days. But, by some miracle, he managed to get permission to extend his leave for ten days before he flew to the Philippines.

He called me all excited, with the news—he had arranged a ticket for me to fly to San Francisco the next morning. I was so ecstatic at the prospect of being with him, if only for a few more days, that I could have flown to San Francisco without the plane. Chase and I made use of every minute of the next few precious days together.

On the flight back to Denver—lulled by the drone of the engines carrying me home—a multitude of thoughts whirled through my mind. *"Whatever happened to my plans for finishing college and then working for some Embassy? Will I ever be able to complete my degree? How is it possible to be so 'one' with another person in both body and in spirit?"*

But, Who's Counting?

Our first baby, a beautiful girl named Emily, named after Chase's mother, was born on Clark Air Force Base in the Philippines. Thank heaven she was not a preemie as we had been married nine months and ten days when she arrived! In those days, I am sure all of my friends' mothers were counting the days after our wedding.

Chase was enthralled with his beautiful new baby girl toy! Her nickname soon became Mia—dad's choice. He loved the name. He would sing lullabies until she fell asleep and then he would sit by her crib and watch her sleep. One of his favorite songs was about scarlet ribbons in her hair.

Do not ask me why that song was so special to him—it just was.

He was so infatuated with the song he spent one day going to every store on and off the base searching for scarlet ribbons to tie on his baby girl's crib. By the end of his search, the only ribbon he could find that was wide enough to suit him was yellow!

Shortly after Mia was born, I went back to college and struggled to finish my education. When someone asks, "Where did you go to college?" I just say, "How long do you have?" Sixteen months after the birth of our little girl, we were blessed with another perfect baby—this time a boy named after his dad—a.k.a. CJ for short.

Between diapers and moving, I managed to fit in studying but it took me four more years instead of three to complete my degree.

Then, as a graduation present to me/us, we had our third child—a daughter nicknamed "Imp." Now, all we needed to fill our requirement was one more boy to even out our foursome.

Since Chase and I had both been only children raised by single parents most of our lives, having several children and a close family was important to us. Call us old-fashioned if you will, but we wanted four children! We wanted two boys and two girls, which was the order we had put into the stork when we first got married.

We wanted to build family traditions that neither of us had had in our own childhood. We wanted our children to have the siblings we never had and a house full of family over the holidays. We wanted lots of children and a St. Bernard to be their nanny. We wanted to watch our children and their children playing soccer on our lawn.

A LITTLE PERSONAL BACKGROUND

Chapter 1
The "Adventure" Begins

One day in mid-December 1963, Chase received his orders. His assignment was for a tour of duty at Incirlik Air Force Base in Turkey. My heart sunk, as we had not been expecting to have to move for at least another year.

Questions started filling my mind. Where the heck is Adana, Turkey? How do you pronounce Incirlik? The answer to the first question was easy—Adana is on the South Eastern part of Turkey close to the Syrian border. Its population was about 789,000.

The most imperative question was, "Could we go, too?" We had a choice to make. He could take an unaccompanied tour, which meant that he would be stationed in Turkey by himself for eighteen months. Or, he could take an accompanied tour and take us with him but that meant we all would be there for two years.

Without hesitation, the accompanied tour was our choice! In our mind's eye, we envisioned Adana to be a modern, European city like Istanbul. However, it only goes to show that one should never assume anything and ones mind's eye can be very wrong.

The two older children could not stop laughing about a country named Turkey. They ran around saying, "Gobble, gobble," off and on for the rest of the day.

Many other wives, I later found out, had said, "Heck,

no!" They were not about to move to Turkey.

Chase was grateful I had taken the attitude that 'this would be an adventure.' We felt it was a good opportunity to educate our two older children, Mia and CJ, age six and five, about life outside the United States. Our baby, Imp, at eleven months, would be too young to remember.

The baby Imp.

I was grateful for the opportunities I had been afforded as both a child and an adult to see the world. I was pleased we could do the same for our little brood.

On the selfish side, I definitely did not want to spend eighteen months away from Chase raising three young children if I did not have to. Notwithstanding, the fact I would miss him terribly!

It was your average overseas military move. The husband relocates first to the new base thousands of miles away under the guise of "finding housing in this faraway land."

This process, as every military wife knows, is actually a scheme instituted many years ago by ancient warriors. It provides the warrior a means of escaping the ordeals of packing, dealing with movers and the transportation of small sometimes, unwilling children to the new and faraway homeland. It soon became the standard relocation procedure in the modern military...The military takes care of their own.

It was not logical to me how warriors who are strong enough to turn back the throngs of invading forces can become weak in the knees when confronted with packing, movers and the physical transportation of small children and diaper bags.

Ah, yes! We then received another dividend—my mother. Mother was coming to help me prepare for the move. As many attributes as Mother had, she was not the person we needed around when trying to move. She always claimed the attention that I needed to give to the children and other tasks. She did not like dealing with babies or toddlers. However, she enjoyed the older children.

She had volunteered to drive our sports car, the XK 150 Jag we were keeping, back to Denver to store during our upcoming tour in Turkey. We were outgrowing our two little sports cars and our old Porsche had seen its better days.

It had become a case of selling some of the children or purchasing a bigger car. It was a toss-up, as both the children and the sports cars were really nifty!

We opted to sell one of the sports cars, the old Porsche, and keep all three children. We conceded and bought a two-year-old Chevy station wagon to take with us to Turkey. (The Government only paid to ship one car overseas anyway.)

We Would Miss Him

Chase left for Turkey on an overcast day in mid-January. He had to drive the station wagon to the Naval Port in New Jersey for shipment.

We hated to see him drive off down the road that grey drizzly day partly because the children and I would miss him so. The counterpart was that I was feeling a bit overwhelmed by all there was to accomplish in the next couple of months all by myself.

I had managed to make the move to the Philippines all alone after Chase and I were married but I did not have children, cars and a house full of furniture to deal with back then.

After Chase left, I spent the next few hours feeling alone and sorry for myself and then decided I had wallowed enough in self-pity. When it stopped raining, I took the children on a walk and picked some oranges from the orange grove by our house with permission from the owner. Then it was time to tuck the children into bed and start making a big list of to do's.

It would probably be at least two or three months before the children and I could make the move to Turkey to join Chase. First, he had to find housing off base for us, which was hard to come by, so they say. My next task was to find a renter for our house, arrange for the movers, and solve all those not so minor little details.

Our relocation sponsor in Turkey told us to bring everything we might need in the way of clothes and especially shoes as things were very limited in Turkey at the Base Exchange.

Sewing was my hobby as well as a necessity with three children. So, I bought lots of material to take along and several sizes of shoes for the children.

Oh, yes! I packed lots of books and games since there was no television station in Adana and we would be living off base for a while. It was a good thing Chase and I liked to play chess when and if we could find the time.

It was essential that we order a few presents for the children for our first Easter and Mia's birthday before leaving for Turkey. It was tough trying to guess what the children might want from the Easter bunny or for Mia's birthday. My attitude was, "They will get what they will get."

Things started coming slowly together for the move. I much appreciated that our neighbors kept a good eye on the children and me. I did not want to bother them if I did not need to but it was comforting to know I could always call on them if we got into a bind.

Several weeks after Chase arrived in Turkey he found us housing off base. This was at least one big hurdle down.

We hoped we would be reassigned back to Orlando AFB after Turkey, so we did not want to sell the house. As any military person knows, the odds of being reassigned to where we actually wanted to go on our return were small...but one can dream.

I made arrangements for the movers to pack and load our household goods in two weeks. Things were going as smoothly as possible until Mia came down with a bad case of the chicken pox. Two days later so did Imp, but so far she had only one pock on her face. *"Oh, Lord, what do I do now?"*

We would not be allowed to travel if Mia's or Imp's chicken pox is not gone by our travel date.

Mia and CJ.

Mother Arrives

I was having about all the fun one person could possibly have the afternoon I picked mother up from the airport. I was also trying to pack, care for a baby and a daughter with the chicken pox, and manage one young son to boot.

She was not in one of her better moods when she arrived. She started in on me two minutes after we gave her a hello kiss. She went on and on about what a bad choice I had made in taking her grandchildren to such a remote place. I was surprised to hear this from "Miss Globetrotter, herself."

Of course, the fact the children and I wanted desperately to be with our husband and father did not seem to hold much weight with her.

It did not take Einstein to realize why Mother had already gone through four husbands. She was much like an Auntie Mame but without a sense of humor.

I knew very well what the real reason was for mother not wanting us to relocate with Chase. She wanted to keep me, her only child, close to her.

Mother had become very jealous of my closeness with Chase—of our oneness. She was jealous of the attention I now had to share with our children. We did everything we could to make her feel part of our family but it was never enough.

Several years ago, before we had children (BC), she wanted me to stay with her instead of joining Chase in the Philippines. Mother had wanted Chase to get out of the Air Force and take over her business. She wanted the 'three of us' to live happily ever after.

Once, when she was in the midst of one of her jealous snits, I tried to explain to Mother my view of love. We were visiting in Denver at the time and she viewed my nightly goodnight call to Chase as an unnecessary waste of money. "Besides you do not call me, your mother, every night when you are home," she said.

I tried to explain, "When someone new comes into your life, it doesn't take away the love you already have for the first person; your heart just gets bigger to take in the love for the new person in your life." I continued, "When you have a new baby, you don't have to stop loving your other children. There's always room for one more."

As you might expect, this example did not go over well with mother. She retorted, "I don't appreciate being compared to a child." I quickly knew I had obviously screwed up and definitely used the wrong analogy.

In spite of the frustration I felt at times due to this very opinionated, independent woman, I had at least learned patience from being her daughter.

As a child, I learned to think about every word that came out of my mouth before I said it. Whatever I said could and would be used against me at some point in time.

At age seven, I once yelled, "I hate you!" Assuredly, I did not mean it but that retort was forever used against me. I learned the concept of cause and effect at an early age. In the end, it became one of the best life lessons I could have been taught, albeit, unknowingly.

I acquired by osmosis from her an inner assurance that a person can accomplish anything one is truly determined to achieve. Actually, my mother had a slightly different word for my inner strength. The word bull-headedness seemed to come up a lot from her as I was growing up...*I wonder where I inherited that trait!*

It is odd my mother would call me bull-headed. This woman, at almost seventy years old and alone, took her last road trip from England to India alone! Mother would not be deterred from traveling in spite of the mere reason the State Department had issued a tourist warning for two of the countries she would be driving through. Instead, Mother bought a Volkswagen camper in England and drove to India by way of Yugoslavia and Afghanistan. She accomplished this at an age when many grandmothers would be sitting on their front porches in their rocking chairs.

I look back now and see how each phase of life prepares us to take on the challenge of the next. What training ground this adventure in the Middle East would consequently turn out to be!

In Retrospect

I had learned valuable lessons from Mother. I learned to respect authority but to not be intimidated by it. With her, I had traveled and lived in foreign countries and felt reasonably at home in different cultures. Without those lessons, I would surely not have been prepared, at age twenty-five, to function in the coming months and years ahead.

I was certain I had learned just about all I would need to know in college! How stupid and naive I was!

If only the colleges I had attended offered a course in "Survival in the Middle East, 101." Believe me, I/we were soon to have the equivalent of a Master's Degree in the subject.

Back to the Move

Mia's chicken pox had cleared up enough to travel. Baby Imp had gotten only one chicken pox on her chin so the base Doc said it was safe to travel.

Mother had left with our little red sports car the day before the movers came to pack and load the furniture. We were on a roll!

The movers came and went. That night our neighbors were so generous—they invited us to stay at their house for the next two days until we were to fly to Turkey. Since our neighbors had six children of their own, it was a very generous offer. How kind they were to take care of the children while I got the house in order for our new renters.

Chapter 2
Attitude and Ladders

Finally, the children and I were on our way to join Dad. The first leg of our journey was from Orlando to New York City and included a seven-hour layover. From New York, we flew to Ankara with a quick change of planes in Italy. Our final destination was Adana, Turkey. Our journey would take us twenty-seven hours including three airplanes and one bus ride.

The bus trip was not in the original itinerary and is a story in its own right!

Thanks to the powers above, Imp slept for almost the entire plane ride from New York to Ankara. The other two children were beyond good!

Our children were quite a contrast to the five children of another military wife who was traveling on our plane. Her children were swinging from the rafters, so to speak, after we left La Guardia. In our opinion, the flight attendant deserved hazardous duty pay!

The mother was French and was married to an Army man. She spoke almost no English. Given that I was the only one on board that spoke any French at all, I took on the task of trying to translate. She had a very different dialect than what I was used to which created a slight problem and made it difficult for me to understand her.

Not only did this poor woman have five children ages eight years to nine months old but she was expecting again. Everyone on the plane was of the opinion that those five came from a gene pool that should not have been allowed to reproduce... Sorry to say—I had to agree.

Up to this point, I had always felt that being a "Military Brat" was rather an honor for our children. However, after meeting those five children I understood from whence the expression might have originated.

As our plane landed in Ankara, you could hear a sigh of relief from all of those poor passengers who were sitting near the brats including the children and me.

After landing, we went into the terminal to have our bags inspected by the customs agent.

Mia had to go to the bathroom. One of the American women from the plane offered to take her. I will admit I was a little apprehensive about letting a stranger take her even though I had a full view of the bathroom door.

I really did not have much choice with all the mass around me plus the two other children. I remained seated with CJ, the baby, and our cumulative pile of luggage.

It was only a minute or so before Mia reappeared. She came running saying, "Mommy they don't have any toilets here and I had to squat and pee into a slot in the ground. I am not going to go to the bathroom ever again until we get back home!" I mumbled to myself, "*You will have a long wait, child.*" The other American woman assured me she felt the same way. She said it was worse than any outhouse she had seen. She had had to hold Mia so the poor child did not fall in the long, rectangular hole. Welcome to Turkey!

I reassured Mia that the house Daddy had found had a real toilet. As I was saying those words, I hoped that was the case, but then again, it was a subject Chase had not actually addressed in his letters. I too now felt concern as well about this subject.

We had another two hours until our next and final flight to Adana. The other American woman and I tried to entertain the children who were starting to get a bit weary of travel.

Alas, a Turkish man came over and informed us we were to follow him to his bus. With children in tow, we pulled all our bags to the waiting military bus. We both questioned a bus trip at this point, but we were assured that it was now necessary. Our first thought was, "Maybe the flight had been canceled."

The children, the other American woman and I sat down in the old bus. It was much too hot to close the windows. The dust poured in as the bus bumped down the road filled with potholes.

We were the only females on the bus—the other passengers were all Army men. They kept looking at us rather strangely, I must say, but no one said a word to either of us.

About twenty minutes into this 'delightful' trip into the Turkish hills, I grabbed onto the backs of the seats and made my way to the driver. "Sir, are you sure this is the way to the Air Force base in Adana?" I queried. "Heck no, Mam!" said the GI sitting next to the driver, "We're going to an Army base in the Anatolian Plains."

About that time, several of the young GIs, realizing the mistake, started joking with us. They said that two females would be very welcome where they were going. They were heading to a remote Army station for a six-month tour where no female dependents were authorized!

The bus driver had to turn around and take us back to the airport... He was not happy.

Then, as if I was not embarrassed enough already, Imp starts calling the GI sitting in front of us, "Dah Dah" and wanting him to hold her! I felt as out of place as a Harvard preppy in a biker bar at this point!

We did make it back to the airport, barely in time, to board the one and only daily flight to Adana.

Welcome to Our New Home

The children and I could hardly wait to reach our final destination. Our trip was almost over with only one more hour to go! Finally, as the sun set over the top of a Mosque, our small plane bounced down out of the sky onto the bumpy tarmac and rolled to a stop at the end of the runway in Adana, Turkey.

I could not believe the pilot actually shut down the engines a few seconds *before* landing, or so it seemed, then allowed the plane to roll to a stop. This was indeed a strange and mysterious land and an even stranger landing procedure.

The pilot and the stewardess then disembarked the plane leaving us, their passengers, to fend for ourselves. This was definitely a no-frills airline. Neither the pilot nor stewardess uttered a word—not even a "Thank you for flying our Airline."

Obviously, landing in front of the small terminal was out of the question. I could only assume the pilot felt we all needed the exercise after our long flights.

Chase later commented he, too, had learned new techniques on his flight into Adana. He had mentioned that perhaps these procedures would best be left out of the pilot's procedural manual.

I looked out the window of the plane as we waited our turn to exit and was ecstatic and relieved to see Chase walking down the runway.

It seemed to take forever for us to disembark. Frustratingly we had to climb over the scattered baggage in the aisle and work our way down the rickety stairs.

Finally, our feet were resting on good old Mother Earth once again.

An open-bed truck came slowly down the runway. I was hoping this would be our transportation to the terminal. Alas, the truck was coming for the luggage not the passengers.

Mia and CJ raced down the runway both jumping up at the same time on their Dad—almost knocking him down. They nearly squeezed the breath out of him with huge, big, bear hugs!

It took me what seemed an eternity to reach Chase's side as I tried to balance Imp and several bags at the same time. This scene definitely was not as romantic a sight as in the movies where two people run in slow motion toward each other, embrace, kiss passionately, and the camera fades.

Now our family was whole. We were, once again, in each other's arms.

An overwhelming sense of serenity, of our oneness, swept over me. My hand was back in my husband's strong but gentle grip and the baby tucked over her father's shoulder—her little blond head snuggled next to his.

We walked to our waiting transportation. Chase had borrowed a car because our station wagon was still a no-show in Turkey.

When the man in the old airport truck finally brought our luggage almost to the terminal, we loaded the car and were off to see our new home.

New Sights and Sounds

The trip to the house would prove to be interesting for us all.

In the time it took to pick up the luggage and load it in the car, the sky had gone from crimson red to dusk and then to dark. There was nonetheless at least some moon to light our way.

Our older children's eyes opened larger than saucers as they took in all the strange new sights, sounds and smells around them.

The thick dust was kicked up from the car's tires as we drove toward town making it hard for us to see at times. The car bounced and bumped until we finally got on to even pavement.

Many of the houses outside of town were made of mud and sticks. Chase told me that many of them had no running water.

You could tell that the people who lived in these houses made every attempt to keep them neat. Even the dirt in front of their house was freshly swept each day. All of the droppings from horses and camels and donkeys were promptly cleaned up.

CJ shouted, "There's Sinbad," when he saw the first Turkish man dressed in his baggy peasant pants. Foreigners refer to these pants as '90-Dayers.' I will leave that to your imagination!

As we neared the main part of town, we could see that many of the little shops were closed. A few outdoor coffee shops and restaurants were still open, as well as the Bazaar which is a Turkish version of a strip shopping center.

A rather large number of families were out strolling for the evening eating ice cream or shaved ice with syrup.

It was their entertainment and they looked quite content.

We passed two cafés with several men in each seated at little tables drinking something red from small glasses. They were deep in conversation.

The few single women we saw walking were not alone. They were with their husbands, children or a female chaperone.

All the older women were wearing black clothing and long black coats even though it was a rather warm evening. Some of the younger women were dressed in more modern attire; they had long skirts and blouses or sweaters with long sleeves. All were wearing scarves on their heads.

Chase and I chuckled when we saw the expression on Mia's face as we passed a meat market that was still open in the Bazaar.

Our car came to a stop and then we had to drive around a *stalled* horse and wagon. There next to us in the meat market hung several lamb carcasses in the open storefront—all lined up waiting to be sold.

The butcher, in an attempt to make the lamb carcasses look more appealing, had placed flowers in all the little lamb's butts! To this day, this is still one of the children's most vivid memories of Turkey!

We subsequently found out those flowers were not there just for cosmetic reasons. Certain flowers mixed in that unique bouquet actually helped keep away some of the flies.

We continued past the Bazaar and downtown area and then onto a newer and more modern street. We drove past the American Consulate, turned onto a cobblestone road and, within blocks; we were pulling up into the dirt driveway of our new home.

And Then We Were Home

There in front of us was a large two-story house with a wide veranda and a very tall thick, cement block fence. It was quite impressive from the outside.

Chase had already written me in part, at least, about the house. We were renting the downstairs and the Landlord and his wife lived upstairs. These were totally separate living quarters, rather like a modern American condominium, or in this case, a not so modern condominium.

Chase had already warned me that the house needed a lot of cleaning but this had been his only choice. It was this place or nothing.

As we entered the house, my heart sank. There was so much to do to make it habitable but I did not have the heart to say a word. I knew Chase had already put a lot of elbow grease into bringing it up to this condition in the days before we arrived.

The floors were all cement, impregnated with a dark brownish red pigment. It had taken Chase the better part of five nights after work to get the dirt and rancid smells out of the house with bleach and water. The rags he used to clean the floors had turned a murky red color as the red pigment in the concrete oozed out at the first contact with water. (The previous renters had left their two dogs in the house for long periods of time).

By now, my excitement in seeing Chase was surpassed by my exhaustion. All I wanted was to have a hot bath, to snuggle down in Chase's arms, and then to fall into blessed sleep.

I would have to be patient. It would take a while for the wood to burn hot enough to warm the water. Yes, the hot water heater was *powered* by wood.

Chase had not had time to start the fire before he went to pick us up. He only had time to buy groceries, drop them off at the house, and race to the airport.

In the bathroom, there was a large, old Turkish bathtub on legs. It was large enough for our entire family. It emptied into a drain that had been chiseled into the cement floor. This allowed the water to vanish through an old rusty pipe at the wall.

The small closet-like room where the wood was now stored for the hot water heater had actually been the Turkish style toilet identical to the one in the Airport at Ankara. You remember—the one which so delighted Mia?

Thank heavens the house had been Americanized, so to speak, with a real toilet, tub, and at least some way to heat water. The bathroom was the only source for hot water and we were one of the few families we knew who actually had this luxury off the Air Force base.

I unpacked while Chase got the water heater fire going. My unpacking consisted of putting a few things on the windowsill and a chair as our furniture had not yet arrived.

Chase had procured cots from family services for the children, a playpen for the baby, a kitchen table, four chairs, a few dishes and, oh, yes, a much appreciated loaned bed from one of the families in Chase's squadron.

A large picnic cooler would have to suffice for a refrigerator. I had packed an electric frying pan in my suitcase that Chase had insisted I bring. He had borrowed a two burner Coleman stove because there was no stove in the kitchen. Luckily, the kitchen did have a flue where the Turkish women cooked on their charcoal stove.

About an hour later, we had all indulged in our first bath in our huge Turkish tub—first the children and then the parents.

Naturally, the children were wide-awake after all the sleeping they had done on the plane.

I, however, had to have some sleep. Chase and the children were left to their own devices for the next few hours with orders not to wake Mom under penalty of death.

Chase would have to put the children to bed and I would have to forgo the luxury of falling asleep in his arms tonight.

As you might deduce, this was not exactly the way Chase and I had planned to spend our first night in Turkey together! Chase had bought champagne and luxurious smelling bath oil and we had planned to spend our first night here, in a somewhat different manner. "*So, maybe sometime by the time the children go to college we can indulge in the bottle of Champaign and use the oil*," I told myself.

The next morning we were awakened by the neighbor's rooster crowing, the clip-clop of horse's hoofs and the rumble of the cart's wheels on the cobblestone road in front of our house.

When I finally came out of the twilight zone of sleep, I had a case of full-blown twenty-four-hour flu.

For the first time in my life, I was thankful for this bug; I now had an excuse to stay in bed for just a few more hours. I was deeply thankful that it was Saturday and Chase was home to watch the children…"*If I live through this flu, I know I am going to love learning about this country.*"

As the cool, soft, morning air carried the scent of the roses into our bedroom from the garden, I was already envisioning what the house would look like painted white with flowers and pretty pictures hung on the wall.

I fell back to sleep feeling achy but somehow very much at home already.

Attitude and Ladders

Our house was located in Adana—some eight miles from the base and a few blocks from the American Consulate. It was in an upper-class Turkish neighborhood some distance from the Little America where most base personnel live across town. (Base housing was very limited, so most of the military personnel lived off base.)

As I mentioned before, the house was a two-family home shared with our Landlord. He was a Turkish doctor. He and his wife lived upstairs and had a separate entrance.

Our Landlord rented the apartment to us as a favor to a mutual friend but only because Chase was also in the medical field. Originally, our Landlord had refused to rent to another American.

We were very grateful that he had been persuaded to change his mind.

Unfortunately, our American predecessor had not been a good tenant and had definitely given us Yanks a poor image in the neighborhood. An image we would work hard to correct.

It was obvious we would have to clean and clean and paint and paint. This was no small feat because the ceilings were sixteen feet high and the plaster peeled off onto the roller as we applied the paint.

We finally got the technique down. We could only roll over the plaster one quick time then let it fully dry before we applied the next coat. It took four coats and two weeks before it was finally covered.

The Turkish tri-pod type ladder made the process even more interesting to complete. The ladder operated more like a pendulum swaying back and forth and back and forth. No matter which way you held your tongue or how hard you prayed to Allah or to God the ladder just kept swaying.

After nights and nights of work, we had finally turned those disgusting dark, dirty, clay red walls into clean white ones. They were now ready for pictures to be hung, if and when, we got our household goods.

On the plus side, we could now add to our resume: "Experienced in Turkish House Painting—101."

By the Bye

Chase—somehow—forgot to mention in his letters that we would not be able to use our washing machine in Turkey. We would need to wash all our clothes in the bathtub because it was the only source of hot water!

He was wise enough to counter the shock of no washing machine with the fact that he would hire a maid to come in three days a week to help do the laundry and cleaning. (Maids were paid twenty-five to thirty dollars a month.)

The upside to this house was that it had a huge covered porch around two sides and a magnificent rose-garden.

A ten-foot high, twelve-inch thick cement wall surrounded the garden. Within those walls grew fifty-six rose bushes and several sweet lemon trees. We were surrounded by both beauty and security for the children.

I highly recommend that when you rent your next house in the Middle East, you rent a house with a covered porch and a high, thick wall. It's a great place for children to play during the rainy season. The high, thick walls are a must for stopping bullets during civil unrest—otherwise known as a coup.

By the way, you don't want to forget to bring your sense of humor with you when moving to the Middle East!

Chapter 3
Learning to Adjust

We were updated on the arrival of our household goods by the Transportation Officer who told us, "Your shipment will not be delivered for another month." In the meantime, we had to make due.

The next notification came again from the same official who said, "Our car will, maybe, arrive in the next few weeks." In truth, it turned out, the car was accidentally off-loaded in Italy and was mysteriously lost. So, we continued to ride the bus to the base.

And You Learn to Adjust

Meanwhile, we all learned to adjust. We soaked in the beauty of the rose garden. We bought wondrous, yummy mysterious melons and fruits that we had never seen or tasted before from the street vendor.

We named the melons what else but mystery melons. We never quite knew what they would taste like inside. Sometimes the melons would look like regular little watermelons outside and taste like honeydew inside. The next time, the same-looking melon would taste completely different. They were always delicious. It always was a fun little surprise.

The street vendor, a well-kept middle-aged looking

man with only a few front teeth, came by the house daily pushing his cart full of produce. It was fun to haggle, Turkish style, over the prices each day. It was a game.

In this part of the world if you did not bargain over the price, you lost respect in your neighborhood and were considered stupid for paying the full price for anything. I had to remind myself to not try this method at Macy's when I returned to the real world!

We began to look forward to the fruit and vegetable man's daily visit. It was not long before he was giving the children or me almost more than we were purchasing. Many days he brought us something special. Sometimes it was a delectable pastry from his wife or a special fruit or vegetable we had never tasted before.

One day he told me that he had a young daughter. We asked if he would mind if we bought her a little something. We bought her a Barbie doll. He was extremely pleased. Now his daughter would be the only child in his neighborhood to have such a wondrous doll. She would be the envy of her peers.

It was difficult at first to get used to not drinking or using water from the faucet. The water was not safe - not even for cooking. We hauled the water from the base in five-gallon cans, which was not an easy task for a family of five, especially without our car.

Occasionally, Chase was able to borrow a friend's car to bring our water and the majority of our weekly groceries from the base to home.

The point of not drinking the tap water was soon brought home to us in a rather vivid manner. One day as we were passing over the river on the way to the base, we saw several dead animals floating down the river—two cows and a lamb to be exact.

The river in which the dead carcasses were normally

dumped, doubled as the city water supply. How quaint! From that day on, we most assuredly did not need a reminder to drink only water we brought from the base.

We Finally Cracked the Aloof Facade

We soon become good friends with several of our Turkish neighbors but we could not seem to crack the aloof façade of our Landlord and his wife.

It was now two days before Easter and still no furniture or car. (We had arrived in early February.) All of us were getting weary of having nothing but the very bare essentials. There were no pictures or vases to put flowers in the house. We had nothing to make the house feel warm and cheery. We needed more kitchenware and most of all we needed the children's stuff.

In an attempt to make our small austere dining room table appear more festive, I knocked on the door and politely asked our Landlord if we might pick four of their beautiful roses and six sweet lemons to make some lemonade.

They agreed this would be acceptable to them. That afternoon while they watched from their upstairs window, we picked exactly four roses and six sweet lemons.

Those four beautiful large roses placed in a drinking glass brightened up our sparse dining room immeasurably.

That night the dinner table was enhanced with the sweet scent of roses, as we ate traditional Turkish food and sipped the marvelous lemonade made from the huge, orange-sized, sweet lemons.

The next day there was a knock on the door. As Mia opened the door she gave a squeal of delight and yelled,

"Oh, Mommy, come here."

There stood our new friends—the Landlord and his wife. Their arms were laden with every rose as well as ripe, sweet lemons from their garden all for us! My heart filled immediately with gratitude and love for these two people and their compassionate gesture.

They had accepted us into their world.

Turkish Landlord & His Wife.

Bless them! They had seen the joy in our faces that the beauty of those four roses had brought to all of us. They were both surprised and pleased we had actually asked for permission instead of simply helping ourselves to their property as our predecessors had done.

The two of them had waited and watched our behavior with reserve for weeks. We had changed the image of the "ugly Americans" in their eyes.

They were soon to become like parents to Chase and me and akin to grandparents to our children.

Our Landlords were most adamant in pointing out that they were from Istanbul and therefore cultured. They insisted they teach us to speak proper Turkish! They were unyielding that we were not to learn the local accent as we were trying to speak the language. According to them, the local dialect was for peasants.

They were very modern by Turkish standards. His wife would normally not wear even a scarf on her head. Upon occasion, she even ventured out without a chaperone. She was quite adventurous for a Turkish woman, I must say.

We felt very blessed that special day. There, in a country that was so anti-American, our neighbors and newfound friends had made us feel so very welcome!

Easter Morn'

We were up as soon as the roosters starting crowing and I made breakfast early. Since the car had not arrived, we had to take the bus to the base to go to Easter services.

Please recall that in order to have hot water we first had to start a fire in the Turkish hot water tank, which always took forever.

That old wood burning hot water tank had a flue pipe that went all the way up and out our sixteen-foot high ceiling. Mathematically, that would make about twelve total feet of pipe that were in three sections. (Retain this information as it will play a role in the following episode.) Be advised that the flue was supposed to have been cleaned of the soot before we took possession of the house.

As any parent knows it is a task to get three young children all dressed up to go anywhere—let alone church!

Our family was on a roll and everyone was fed. Parents and children were clean and dressed and ready to walk out the door. We headed to the bus stop that was only a few blocks away. ...*So far so good!*

As any woman knows, having to walk over cobblestones in high heel shoes is not an easy feat. (*Sorry for the pun.*)

As Murphy's Law would have it, we were three blocks from the house when one of my heels broke. I handed the baby to Chase and told him to go on. He was to wait for me at the bus stop.

For the first half a block I tried taking off both shoes but the cobblestone hurt my feet and tore my nylons. The alternative was to put both shoes back on and hobble home to get my only other pair of heels. At home, it became a race to find my last pair of nylons, locate another pair of shoes, then sprint back to the bus stop before the bus arrived.

Either Mr. Murphy or the devil was testing me because just before I reached the bus stop another heel broke on that pair of shoes. I had no choice now because the bus was just turning the corner. I would need to board now or we would all miss church.

I prayed all way to the base that we could find a seat at the back of church. When we finally walked in, naturally, the only open seating for the five of us was in the very front row.

I tried to walk as normal as possible down the middle aisle, trying desperately not to look deformed.

Halfway through church, the chaplain motioned for the parishioners to take our seats. Mia said "sit" loud enough for everyone to hear. Chase and I could have slithered under the pew with embarrassment. Mia's "sit" sounded exactly like the 'S' word.

After church, we went to the BX and I bought a pair of flat-heeled shoes to wear on our way back to the house. By this time, I was more than frazzled and my Easter spirit had definitely waned.

As Chase unlocked the front door there was a sigh of relief from this mom...*Ah, relaxation at last!*

Mia and CJ scurried to get their play clothes on while we changed ours and the baby's.

Then, came the pièce de résistance of our perfect day. Chase and I headed to the bathroom to wash our faces and behold what should we find but black, thick, soot all over the room. That twelve-foot flue had fallen down and come apart in all three places pouring out their black grungy contents...

I will not even discuss the 'fun' we had cleaning up that disgusting mess!

It was an Easter to remember!

Wheels Again

Finally, our car was located and loaded onto a ship with the final destination to be Turkey, or so they told us.

I could hardly wait to have wheels again and not have to ride the bus. As you can imagine trying to ride the bus with three children in tow and a lap full of shopping bags did not make for fun-packed days.

The car was scheduled to arrive on the next ship and was due to dock in Turkey in a week. Chase would have to go to the port and sign papers to take possession.

Two weeks later, when the car did finally arrive at port, Chase and I both went down to pick it up.

It had been over three long months since Chase had taken it to port for transport to Turkey.

We could not have been happier to see our two-year-old station wagon than if it had been a new Ferrari even though it was covered in grunge.

Our once blue station wagon was now brown with layers of dirt and sea salt. It obviously had been sitting on a dock for a very long time. After Chase took official possession of it, we asked where we could have the car cleaned and washed.

That comment got a big grin from the Sargent as he pointed to an area that had a plain old hose. We rinsed off the scuzzy grime as best we could.

We now had a clean car but we were left with muddy clothes for the trip back to the house.

In spite of looking a bit grungy ourselves, we went to one of the little cafes by the water for a bite of their wonderful fish and pilaf. The owner took one look at us and gave us a table at the very back of the café!

Cars n' Planes

Back in the States, Chase and I had raced and rallied our two sports cars for several years on weekends. I loved to hear the purr of the Abarth, racing exhausts, when we drove flat out. Actually, I loved anything with a motor that made a lot of noise and roared!

Driving was in our blood. My birth father had been a B-24 pilot in WWII. His plane was shot down and he and his crew were all lost in the waters off Burma when I was a wee tyke.

Chase and I shared a love for sports cars and flying. I had just qualified for my own pilot's license when we got orders to leave for Turkey.

I probably would not be an acceptable Moslem wife. *Oh, darn.*

Rock Allergies

The delight I felt over my regained mobility and freedom was shattered a few days after we got the car.

The first time I attempted to drive the children to the base I was thwarted.

People had tried to convince me that Turkish women did not drive cars.

"Well, fine," I said, "I am an American and American women do drive cars! This is not ancient times for heaven's sake, it's the 60's."

After several attempts were made by Turkish (male) drivers to run me off the road and numerous gestures that were their equivalent of our middle finger salute, I decided to leave the driving to Chase or the bus driver for the remainder of our tour.

"If a woman driver upsets these men in Turkey, can you imagine how the sight of a female pilot would flip their Bic?"

I took some solace in the fact that at least we had our bikes to ride. That is, if our household goods ever arrived.

It turns out that women in Turkey should not try to ride bikes, either. Mia and I learned the hard way. She and I decided to go bike riding around our neighborhood one day. Naturally, we put on pants. We were not five blocks from home when several Turkish men and women started yelling and throwing stones at both of us—never mind that Mia was a little girl.

She and I were both terrified we were not going to make it home in one piece. I was furious they would actually put a little girl in such jeopardy.

We quickly learned we are allergic to rocks. They made welts shortly after impact and changed the color of our skin.

Henceforth, Mia and I gave up bike riding as a means of exercise while off base in Turkey. In this case, cowardice truly was the better part of valor.

I hated the fact that I and the other women were treated like second or third class persons in this land. Even the darn neighbors' roosters were given more respect. But then again, this was the Middle East and the rooster is a male.

A Bit of Status

At least I had a *bit* of status in this culture; I was the mother of a son...*Tongue in cheek.* At times I found myself looking at my husband and my son as somehow being part of the enemy camp—members of a fraternity who were stealing my daughter's and my freedom, for they were, of course, male.

Other military wives admitted they, too, had the exact same thoughts and frustrations!

All jokes aside, Chase, dear man, was one of the biggest supporters for women's equality I knew. He loved the fact I shared his passion for cars and planes.

Most of all, he did respect my position as his wife and mother of his children as well as his best friend and partner. Chase was not above washing a bathtub full of diapers when we had no washing machine or cooking dinner on the weekend. *"Now if only I could get him to pick up his clothes as well."*

Our Stuff

Our household goods arrived and it was wonderful to finally, have our belongings or at least most of them.

One full container of our possessions was slightly modified. A four thousand-pound printing machine had been dropped on the side of the container—or so we were told.

Our air conditioner, for example, had been

compromised, shall we say, on one side. It still poured out enough cool air when we plugged it in to keep our house reasonably comfortable. Since the outside temperature many times rose to 116 degrees, believe me, even a slight differential was appreciated.

Our young-ones were much more appreciative of all their toys after doing without. These, the same toys they had become so complacent about back home in the States, now became most precious to these little people.

As they scurried to open up the boxes, I leaned over to Chase and said, "Absence makes the heart grow fonder even when it's a Tonka Toy."

He chuckled as he went off to open up his own box of toys—his tools.

Chapter 4
A Trip to Heaven and Hell

A Summer of Many Sights and Delights

During the next few months our family spent time doing local tourist things.

We barbecued with our nearest American families—a Doctor and his wife (Joe and Sue) whom we considered good friends. They lived across a large field about a quarter of a mile away as the crow flies.

We met a lovely couple named Sam and Mary who had a son the same age as our CJ. Conveniently, our children could play because they lived only a few blocks away.

We felt these were precious days given to us. We had time to absorb as much of the history and mysteries of this country as we could—a history of which was almost too abundant for our minds to grasp.

Because there was no television, we had the perfect opportunity to read and play chess and other games with our two older children.

Our Turkish tub was wonderful. Chase and I bathed the children in it each night. Then put them to bed and read them their bedtime story. Chase would refill the tub and the two of us would spend a long time just soaking and sharing the day's events.

We wondered what it must have been like for those who had lived in this part of the world so many years ago. We envisioned all the wars and loves that had been won and lost on this ancient ground.

There was a practical side to sitting in the tub. It was chilly in winter some nights and we had no central heat. However, we did have a very large kerosene heater that was centrally located in the dining room, which warmed most of the house. It kept the children's room warm but ours got a wee bit chilly.

A Turkish School

Our Turkish friend's wife was a teacher in one of the private schools. She took Mia and CJ with her to school on most Saturdays. Unlike our American schools, the Turkish schools were in session six days a week including Saturdays, which met for only half a day.

The children loved to attend because they were afforded an opportunity that other military children did not have. They learned much more about the culture than their American peers.

We were pleased they had become reasonably conversant in the Turkish language in a very short time. The Turkish children treated Mia and CJ like royalty and for certain, they delighted in the attention.

That Summer We Climbed Castles in the Sky

We climbed up to several old abandoned medieval fortresses high on hills and picnicked on Turkish fare. A typical Turkish picnic consisted of Turkish bread, cheeses, huge black wrinkled Turkish olives, hard-boiled eggs, seltzer or bottled water and delicious fresh peaches.

On one terribly hot and dusty day, we climbed up to Yilan Kalesi on the Anatolian Plain. Because the architects deliberately hid the entrances from the oncoming enemy, it was a challenge trying to find the front entrance to these old fortresses. We were exhausted when we finally gained entrance.

Castle Yilan Kalesi.

At one particularly frustrating fortress, we gave up trying to find the front door. We scaled rocks and a wall before we finally climbed through a window. Once inside, it was difficult for us to find our way back out.

We could imagine what it must have been like in war to have hot oil poured down on top of you or flaming arrows shot in your direction, as you were climbing up the hill to gain entrance.

We could almost feel the presence of the people who had been there before us so many years ago.

The castle was in ruins. The roof had disintegrated long ago and the place had been gutted over the years. It was still exciting to think that deep down in the cistern there might still be treasures!

By the end of the day, we all were exhausted. Both parents and children had an incredible rush from the sense of adventure and achievement.

A Weekend to Remember

Another extraordinary opportunity was presented to us a few weeks later when our friends offered to babysit our children. They wanted Chase and me to have a few days to ourselves.

Chase and I were elated to have a few days without children as most parents well know. We had spoken before about camping out at the old ruins of Cleopatra's Bath and now, was our marvelous opportunity.

Yes, this was the very place where Cleopatra and Mark Anthony had one of their rendezvous so many years ago in their famous Turkish cove.

Chase and I were the only people there. We wallowed in the beauty and the history. We swam through the glistening blue-green waters and around the old Roman columns by day.

Cleopatra's Baths.

We basked in the romance of the moonlight shining down on us by night. It felt almost too perfect to be real.

Here we were—a man and a woman very much in love—with no children and three days all alone in such an ancient, romantic place! What precious time to wallow in our *oneness*.

I might add we tried our best to follow in our predecessor's, Cleo and Mark's, footsteps. In addition, we were not encumbered by the barges and all that nosey, entourage to invade our privacy! In this case, we felt there was a definite upside to being common folk.

We toasted our champagne to Cleo and Mark several times in fact!

Instant Friends

Shortly after our weekend at Cleo and Mark's place, we were introduced to a Turkish man and his wife with whom we became instant friends. We shared many stories of each other's homelands. Our friends had both been well educated abroad.

We later learned that they were members of one of the most prominent families in the country.

Chase and I could never have predicted that in the next year these newfound Turkish friends would be instrumental in trying to help save Chase's life.

Our friend's family was of old Turkish nobility and quite wealthy. The elder father, the head of their family, insisted there must always be twenty-seven people at his dinner table. As a result, many a night we were beckoned to go to his house for dinner.

All of the family members were caring and extremely interesting people. They loved to learn about our country. They wanted to know about the latest fads in America.

They were fascinated with President Kennedy and his

wife and wanted to know what they were like. They asked us questions about the Kennedy's as if we were supposed to know them personally!

Even though the elder father and mother were not fluent in English, they pretended to understand what we were saying. The younger generation spoke English and several other languages quite proficiently.

One night, the elder father decided to give a dinner in our honor. It was very formal and there were more than twenty-seven people.

Chase and I had been studying the culture and trying to learn *proper* Turkish etiquette for the event. One custom was the serving of a soup that was considered quite a delicacy and honor for it to be made for us.

On the evening of the dinner, we were treated royally by our hosts and served the special soup. In front of us was a bowl of clear broth with a lamb's eyeball floating in the middle. Turkish etiquette would dictate that one must swallow the entire eyeball in one gulp or offend the host!

Somehow, Chase and I managed to accomplish the task without throwing up. I pretended it was a raw oyster (which I can't stand either) but the thought of an oyster was much less offensive than that of an eyeball. To this day, I can't look a lamb directly in the eye without my stomach getting queasy!

During that same dinner, our host learned that the maid Chase had hired had worked for us for about two months and then one day never showed up again. She had stolen a few dollars from the children's piggy bank and some of my jewelry. My jewelry was not expensive except for my class ring which was solid gold and had precious stones. She had taken my Girl Scout and Brownie pins and several items I wanted to give to the girls. Our friends tried to locate her with no result.

Our friend's father was appalled that we now had no one to help. They had nine housekeepers in their household. He insisted that one of their maids named Amina, an older family servant, come to work for us the next day.

Amina was just that—older. So, most of the time, I tried to get things done before she came to work. We did not dare suggest we find someone else to replace her because our friend would be insulted. Amina had been with their household for years and was very dear to all of their family.

Amina, sweet woman, treated us all as if we were her children, which was rather nice. She made wonderful baklava, which took all day by the time she rolled out all the many layers of dough. She insisted I do nothing while she was there.

The truth was, I really needed the rest as I had been working hard the day before to get everything done before she stepped foot in the door...*"I am not exactly sure this was the way the maid thing was supposed to work!"*

Amina would have a fit if she saw any of us walking barefoot on the cement floor. She kept telling us we would get a cold and die! She did not speak much English but her sign language quickly got the point across. She came to our house three days a week. The other days, I will admit, we did sometimes go barefoot.

The Muslims religion does not allow their followers to eat pork. One night I had cooked a pork roast for dinner and put the leftovers in the refrigerator. On the next day, Amina, thinking it was chicken ate the remainder, which was normally okay for her to help herself.

Later that afternoon she commented to me, "Madam, your chicken was good." I did not have the heart to tell her it was pork because she would have literally gotten sick.

Imp, our baby, was her favorite. I occasionally dreaded the days Amina came to work, since Imp, usually quite well disciplined for a child her age, knew she could get away with anything when Amina was around.

We, the parents, were not allowed to discipline her in any way—not even a "no" or that parental "evil eye look." Amina would stop us with, "No, madam, Bebek kiymetli," meaning Imp was a precious baby.

Heaven and Hell

Our next outstanding excursion was with our newfound Turkish friends. They took Chase, me and our two oldest children to another amazing historical place.

We traveled to a location not far from Salifke, about one hundred miles from Adana, and only a few miles from the coast of the Mediterranean.

Port City of Iskenderun.

Most Americans stationed at the base never attempt to get out and see some of these historical places. None of the Americans we knew had ventured out past Adana or to the port city of Iskenderun, let alone climb castles.

We drove to a site they called Heaven and Hell. It consisted of two gigantic natural chasms—the first of which is known as Cenet Deresi in Turkish. It contains the ruins of an Armenian chapel dating back to the thirteenth century.

We were somewhat apprehensive about the steep downhill descent on donkeys—especially for the children. Our friends and guide assured us we would be safe. The thought, *"Easy for them to say,"* ran through my mind.

In the early 1900's, The Ottoman Empire committed mass genocide against the Armenians who they considered a danger to their Empire. Men, women and children were brutally murdered. Some Armenians who could not escape to Syria or other countries hid in Heaven and Hell for months.

We rode the donkeys down a long winding path that seemed to disappear into the chasm of the earth. As we followed our guide to the bottom, our legs grew numb from gripping on so tightly around the donkey's belly. In most places, we could not even see the sky due to the overhanging rocks.

Heaven and Hell.

When we finally reached the bottom, hundreds of feet from the surface of the earth, we could not help but marvel at the structure that was before us.

At the entrance to the grotto, hidden under an imposing rock arch, was a chapel. Behind the chapel was a beautiful little stream flowing ever so gently at our feet, with delicate blue flowers and moss growing by its rocky sides.

For us, it was a welcome respite to sit by the stream and take in the sights around us. For the many Armenians who sheltered here, it had meant life or death to them.

Heaven and Hell Chapel.

Armenian inscriptions on the chapel's old, decaying, wooden door were still barely visible.

The roof had fallen in and the wood had been carted away for firewood many years before. Traces of old faded paintings were still visible on the walls.

We were on hallowed ground and it touched our souls. We thought of the people before us that feared for their lives while sheltered in this place, praying for their families to be spared.

After sharing food our guide had brought for us, we all climbed on our donkeys and headed out. Our way back up from the grotto was a little less rigorous than our descent—to say the least. The path was unfortunately still steep but at least we could lean forward in order to keep from sliding off the donkey's back.

Our children and their parents were extremely relieved when we finally reached the summit of our long, endless, ride back up.

A Gypsy Camp

During that same summer, on one of our outings and just before dusk, we spotted gypsies about to stopover for the night. We were fascinated as we watched them set up camp. It turned out to be quite an education in efficiency.

The women unloaded everything off the camels. The women set up camp while the men did the 'hard work' of taking the camels to the watering hole to drink. The men, however, did collect any dry camel dung they found on the ground to use for fuel for the cooking fires.

The women proceeded to toss out tent stakes, which landed within inches of where they needed to be. Then, those poor tired women went about tugging and pulling on the ropes to raise the tents. Next, they lifted and hauled all their Persian rugs inside.

After the women had fed the men, eaten and cleaned up, they had the 'privilege' of working on the rugs. It could take many years to make a single handmade rug if the rug was large. The average rug took two years to make.

Babies and Trains

Amazingly, we saw babies being born of peasant women who were working in the fields. The women wore large skirts or big baggy Turkish pants. When the birth was to be, the woman simply squatted and delivered her baby and then pulled it up out from underneath her bulky skirt.

Though I had birthed three children myself, it made me feel like some kind of a pathetic wimp in comparison.

The following weekend we took a trip on a very old Turkish railroad. It was dusty and hot as most summer days are in the Anatolian Plain. As to be expected, the smoke from the coal-burning engine stunk.

The train's route was short and it would only take a few hours to get to a little village at the end of the line. On our way, we were told the train would be traveling close to the Syrian border.

The Turkish people in the little village were surprised to see foreigners when we arrived. They kindly offered us fresh fruit, Turkish flatbread and bottled soda for our return journey. They would not accept even one Turkish lira.

One young boy spoke a little English. He was delighted to have the opportunity to show off his skills in front of his fellow townsmen.

Immediately, he took on the role of being our interpreter! We did our best to make him look good in front of his townsmen by pretending he was most proficient in English. The truth was, we could hardly understand a word he uttered in our English language.

The engineer blew the train's whistle signaling it was time to leave. We said our goodbyes to our interpreter and his friends and climbed back aboard.

On the return trip, the engineer let Mia and CJ help drive and blow the whistle. They had a ball. He had offered to let Imp blow the whistle, too, but she wanted nothing to do with him.

He did, I will admit, look a little rough. He was unkept, his teeth were yellowish brown and when he smiled, you could see his three, missing teeth. To be exact, had you put him in pirate clothes, he would have been a perfect match.

By the time we got home that night, we were covered with a light coating of soot and grime. We all had sore bottoms from the train's hard wooden seats, but what a unique experience we had.

It was a race to the bathtub for us all. The children wanted to wash up first. Of course, the little urchins won.

Basking in the Sun

We spent several weekends camping and basking in the sunshine on the beach near Karatas some thirty miles from Adana. We taught the children how to snorkel in the magnificent blue-green waters of the Mediterranean.

Chase and I put Mia and CJ in the station wagon to sleep. We slept in a little tent with Imp backed up to the car for security.

Upon arrival at the beach, we were guided to a small out of the way cove where our Turkish friends had insisted we should set up camp. They had assured us that it was both beautiful and a very safe place to stay overnight.

Little did we know then that they had one of their family members, a local police officer, looking out for us the entire time!

Once in the cove, we saw no one the entire weekend. There was nary a person to give Mia and me grief about being females and wearing bathing suits in a public place. Mia and I were cautious. As soon as we got out of the water, we immediately put on long-sleeved sundresses just to be safe.

Chapter 5
Our Son Was Missing

Things Were About to Change

The fun, romantic times would quickly disappear. We were to first face ransom and revolution as a pre-cursor to our hell. We were to face Turkish civil unrest and a coup d'état in the next few months. Next the horror of having our son kidnapped. Still, all of these experiences were just precursors of what was to come.

Children Were at a Premium

Several years before we arrived in Turkey an American couple had their twin daughters, age six, kidnapped. To our knowledge, they never got their precious daughters back.

In Turkey, especially in the villages, the average Turkish death to birth rate at this time was about thirty percent, meaning only thirty percent of all babies born actually survive. The rate is even worse if you include the Kurdish and Gypsy nomadic tribes who sometimes steal children.

According to what several of the local doctors reported in these nomadic tribes, only one baby out of every forty born lives past two years old. Because of the lack of medical facilities and the Muslim tradition, Turkish women and especially babies are at great risk. The average doctor's office has less than a dozen medical instruments of vintage design. They have no access to the normal vaccines like DPT, etc. These numbers included the general population in the towns and villages in the remainder of the country but they did not include Istanbul.

We visited our Landlord's office one day. He was a very prominent and well-respected pediatrician in his community.

The office contained one small wooden table, two straight back chairs, and a wooden cabinet that was about fourteen inches wide and four feet high. The cabinet contained a small tray of instruments including a few pairs of scissors, some old tweezers, and a flat metal stick that he would use for a tongue depressor.

The cabinet also contained a small flashlight and a very old stethoscope. That was just about his entire inventory save for some cotton balls, bandage materials, a bottle of iodine and blood pressure cuff.

In the Muslim world, men would not ever consider allowing their wives to be seen by another man—not even by a doctor who could save her life. Obviously, one can now see why the death to birth rate of children is so high. You can imagine why children, especially healthy pretty ones, were at a premium. Not only were our children healthy but they still had blond hair. They were definitely a rarity in this part of the world.

The two twin girls that had been kidnapped were adorable and blond like Mia and Imp!

Our Son was Missing

It was a lovely morning and a special date for Chase

and me. We had not planned to go anywhere but just have a relaxing day with our little family. We might perhaps have a bit of bubbly and music after our little ones were tucked in for the night.

As I started to cook breakfast, Mia and CJ asked permission to go out and play on the porch. The children knew they were not allowed to go beyond the wall surrounding our house, as it would have been too dangerous.

Mia came back into the house. CJ wanted to stay outside to watch a big truck unload dirt in the field next door. CJ was really into dump trucks and had already put in his order to Santa for one next Christmas. (It takes a long time for Santa to get presents to Turkey and he did not want to take any chances on Santa not getting it made on time.)

After I had finished preparing our bacon, eggs and the wonderful mystery melons, Chase asked Mia to please go get her brother. She returned to tell her Dad that CJ was not on the porch, not in the rose garden, not any place to be found. Chase went out to look for himself.

Like any cook—I was getting annoyed; the eggs were getting cold.

Chase could not find CJ; he knocked on the door of our Landlord to see if perhaps they had invited CJ up to visit. This would have been most unusual as CJ had never gone anywhere without first asking permission. He was not upstairs at our Landlords'.

We looked again around the outside of the house—no CJ.

The truck was gone and only a huge pile of dirt and rock remained.

Chase checked the Turkish neighbors while I ran over

to Sam and Mary's house who were the closest Americans. They also had a son CJ's age but CJ was not there.

On the way home, I looked for CJ in every conceivable place I could possibly imagine between their house and ours. I hurried home hoping he was back at the house but, I did not find our little son.

Chase and I started to feel sick inside. As a parent, somehow you get that feeling in your gut when your instincts tell you your child is in danger.

Chase and I looked at each other. We did not have to say a word; we knew what we had to do next.

We ran outside and started digging. We were terrified that CJ had gone out of the gate and that he might be under the huge dark pile of dirt dumped by the blue and red truck!

If this were so, we would only have minutes. Or, was it already too late?

Our neighbors and Landlord joined in to help us. We all dug frantically!

As we clawed and dug, it was all we could do to keep back panic. We had to choke back the thought of what we possibly could find in any second!

We dare not use shovels for fear of hurting CJ if he was there, beneath that black soil.

As we reached the bottom of that pile of dirt, thank God, our CJ was not there. Shaking, all six of us leaned back and let the tears of relief roll down our cheeks. Our hands were bleeding from the rocks in the dirt and our eyes were caked with mud from wiping the tears away.

We went back into the house to clean up and take care of our torn hands. We washed our faces and hands and put on fresh clothes.

As soon as we could, we rushed upstairs to telephone the base from our Landlord's phone. They informed us they had no authority off base. The "*best*" they could do was to get his description and if anyone were to spot him they would let us know.

Our Landlord called the local police but they were not much help either. Our Turkish neighbors, dear hearts, continued looking for him until dark.

I stayed home in case someone called while our Landlord and Chase drove around searching for CJ, hour after hour to, no avail!

That night Chase and I took turns holding Mia close to us. Our poor little girl was as desperate to see her brother, as were we.

Mia and CJ had always been very close. For example, if one of them was over at a friend's house and was offered a cookie he/she would always ask politely for one to take home to the other.

That agonizing long night came and went—no CJ, no precious son. My arms ached to hold him close again.

The following morning, a woman brought a note and gave it to our Landlord's maid. The note read:

"*Lost boy can be foundes for American mony of 500dl.*"

The ransom money of five hundred dollars was about one and one-half to two years' salary for the average worker in Turkey.

At least the note gave us confirmation, we hoped, that CJ was still alive!

They Found Him

That morning, our Landlord called a meeting of all the doctors in the town. They began to search block by block for the red and blue truck that Mia had seen dumping the dirt in the field next to the house. This was no small job as almost all of the trucks in Adana area were blue and red. Near midafternoon, our Landlord received a call saying CJ had been located and he was unharmed.

CJ was Found!

Our Landlord and his wife who had become like grandparents to our children immediately started crying. I am not quite sure who was bawling the hardest—them or us.

Our Landlord insisted he was the one to go get CJ. An hour later our Landlord brought CJ home to a very, very relieved and grateful family!

The abductors, the men in the red and blue truck, had taken him to a fur factory. CJ was safe, confused and a little scared. But, at least, he had no realization of being in danger or that he had been held for ransom.

Apparently, what had happened was the men lured CJ away from our front gate by asking him in Turkish if he would like a ride. He said, "No, Mommy won't let me." One of them had come in the gate, gone around the corner and came back saying, "Mommy said *tamum*," which meant, "okay."

At least they had been kind to him. He had been well fed and when it came for bedtime they again said, "Mama said it was *tamum* to stay with them over-night." His captors told him they would show him fun the next day and he could ride more in the truck.

Later, we asked our Landlord what the Turkish authorities would do to the men who took CJ. Our Landlord firmly said, "*They* will be taken care of in the Turkish way and they would not be any trouble to anyone again."

Our Landlord's voice was suddenly stern in his response to me when I asked for more detail about "The Turkish way." I knew to query him no more.

The Coup D'état

The word was out that there would be an attempted coup soon. Military personnel were advised unofficially to arm themselves and go home to their families if their families were off base. The rest of the military personnel were restricted to base.

The consulate, which was only a few blocks away from our house, had moved their staff to a more secure location. Only the Turkish military guards remained to protect the building, if necessary. The building had no walled fence around it and was located on the corner of a busy street, which could make it vulnerable.

Normally, military personnel that had guns had to secure them on base unless they were hunting boar. It is important to comment, we had all the proper registration for our two rifles. We did go boar hunting with our American friends, Sue and Joe, several times.

That day, I imagined the base was busy issuing gun licenses for the men who had families off base, so they would be legal.

It was illegal for Turkish civilians to possess firearms. Curiously, many Turkish men had firearms they had made from pipes.

We remained locked in our house with the shutters closed for nearly two days. We could hear gunfire pops occasionally in the distance. We were extremely thankful for the construction of our house with its thick walls and tall fortified outer cement block fence.

Then, the noise in the distance stopped and within hours, we received a message from the base via our Landlord's telephone. The attempted coup was over as quickly as it had started and life went on as usual, or so it would seem on the surface.

There was to be only one sign that anything overt had taken place in Adana. As we drove out to the base the following day, we saw the bodies of two men hanging on the bridge.

Adana Bridge.

Chase and I quickly distracted the children's attention to the other side of the bridge as we crossed only feet away from the lifeless, bloodied bodies. My face turned white as I turned my head and looked back!

From that moment on, I realized this beautiful place was filled with more impending danger than we had realized or wanted to admit.

The vision of those two poor men haunted me for nights, as well as each time we crossed that bridge.

I wondered what they had done that was so wrong, if anything, to end their lives like this. I wondered what their families must have been going through. I wondered if they had children who were asking, "Where is daddy." I worried about two mothers and fathers grieving for their sons!

Secured in our house, I had been worried, of course, but somehow, this attempted coup seemed removed from us. Maybe I simply had a false sense of security. I guess I had a false sense of safety because we were Americans and we therefore had some kind of immunity.

I felt safe knowing Chase was there to protect us. Knowing we had Turkish friends seemed to give me a feeling of security as well, albeit, ever so misguided.

I was assured by Chase that he felt no such sense of security.

I look back on our trip to Heaven and Hell with our Turkish friends and realize the importance of what they had said. On that memorable day, as we were picnicking at the bottom of Heaven and Hell, our friends had strongly recommended to Chase that it might be prudent for him to send his family to safety back in the United States.

Our friends did not realize that once dependents had moved to Turkey, they were obliged to stay for the complete time of the deployment. Our going home was not an option.

At the time, we had no concept of how serious our friend was about the dangers that would be looming for Americans!

A Stolen Car

We had just come back from another camping weekend at the beach with Mia and CJ. The gas tank was almost empty but Chase and I agreed that we were all too tired to drive all the way out to the base to fill it up. He would fill the tank on his way to work.

So, when we arrived home, we cleared out all of our gear from the car, swept out the sand, and locked the car doors.

Chase got the two sandy little urchins bathed and into their pajamas. I made dinner and tried to deal with a tiny little girl who had been spoiled for the past few days by our Landlord and his wife.

The next morning, Chase and I walked out of our front door to say good-bye. It took us a minute to realize our car was gone!

We walked out the front door, down the steps and through the gate. We found ourselves standing where the car should have been until it sunk in—our car had been stolen!

Chase and I were dumbfounded.

I went into the house to take care of the children, while Chase went upstairs to use the phone.

Our Landlord called the local Turkish police to report the missing car and Chase called the base registration office.

He did all he could do and then he took the bus to the base.

Turns out, we were lucky that we had not filled the gas tank the night before. The car was located five days later hanging part way over a cliff in the mountains between Adana and Ankara. Our car had run out of gas!

Apparently, the thieves had broken the small window on the passenger's side to gain access to our car. Then, they had hot-wired the ignition to get it started. After the car had run out of gas, the thieves had not set the brake when they abandoned the car. It rolled across the narrow road and wound up in that precarious position.

One of the local farmers tied a rope around the bumper to stabilize it with his tractor while another truck pulled it back onto the road.

The thief or thieves were evidently going to take our car to Ankara or Istanbul to use it as a taxi. We were told that this was a frequent happening. In this case, I guess they could have named it, "Blue Cab Company," as our station wagon was blue.

With the car having been stolen, we now faced several problems. First, there was the difficulty of not having transportation either for Chase to get to work or for us to get to the base. The only option was to take that darn bus.

Second, we could not run down to our local Turkish Chevy dealer and pick up a new or used automobile.

Third, and worst of all was the Turkish taxes called Baynami. These large taxes were required on any item you brought into the country but did not take when you left.

Each item we brought into Turkey had to be listed— each iron, lamp or table. Electrical and mechanical items were charged a premium and commanded a very high tax in comparison to its original cost.

If your hair dryer gives out you had better hang on to it and plan to ship it back to the good old U. S. of A.

When foreigners left the country, the authorities meticulously checked the list. If you did not have the item/s, you would need to pay the tax.

You can understand our worry when the car was missing. We were faced with paying the tax of over five thousand dollars, which was a lot of money for us.

Chase had to go and retrieve the car so he asked our Turkish friend if he would go with him. Having a person who was Turkish with him turned out to be invaluable. The farmer, who had found the car, spoke no English.

Chase gave the farmer money for his kindness and work in saving our car. It took Chase, the farmer and our Turkish friend some time to get the starter wiring back in working order. Chase was smart enough to have taken his toolbox certain he would have some work to do.

We were deeply thankful to have it back. As you can see, having a car stolen if you are a foreigner in Turkey, had more far-reaching ramifications than in the states. There were usually, no excuses from having to pay the taxes on missing items—with one exception!

The one exception to the Baynami rule was that the man inspecting your household goods required a bribe whether there were missing items or not. Usually, the cost to have your shipment's contents approved would cost some type of household item—not money.

Kennedy has been Assassinated

The sky had finally cleared up after days of rain. The rainy season had started early in November—a month before the normal season of December or January.

It was the Saturday before our first Thanksgiving in Adana. Our turkey was in the refrigerator to thaw and pumpkin pie and whipped cream awaited us.

We decided to take a short drive out of town if the roads were not too muddy. The children were relieved to be able to go somewhere and any destination would do for them.

I packed us a lunch, threw in an old bedspread to sit upon if we could find a place to picnic and we headed to the car. As Chase started to back out of the drive, I turned on the radio to the one English speaking station.

Stunned, he stopped the car! Neither of us could believe the news, President Kennedy had been shot!

We sat in our driveway and listened to the BBC news reporter, hanging on his every word, trying to glean any information we could.

The information was sparse. All that was forthcoming was that he had been shot while riding in a motorcade in Dallas. Mrs. Kennedy was with him in the convertible but she was not hit. President Kennedy had been pronounced dead at the hospital.

Considering the time difference between Turkey and the States and the fact we had not had the radio on, it had been almost twenty-four hours since our President had been assassinated.

It was at this time we realized how far away from home we were.

A dreadful feeling of loss came over both Chase and me.

We were shocked that someone had not gotten in touch officially with the military members off base to tell them of the news.

The news reporter affirmed that Vice President Johnson had been sworn in as the new President but beyond that, we had no intel.

We decided to continue on the outing that we had promised the children.

About twenty minutes into our drive, we decided to turn back. Not knowing what the ramifications might be from Kennedy's assassination for Americans in this foreign country, we were concerned.

The relationship with the United States and Turkey over the Cyprus crisis was escalating. The question in our minds was what would President Johnson's policy be now?

Kennedy and the U.N. had managed to help keep the 'lid on the boiling pot' of Cyprus but the new diplomatic approach might not be the same.

Chase thought it best to go to the base and check the status out with his commander for he was certain all Officers would need to report for duty.

On our way, we stopped to see our friends to ask if they had heard the news but they had not. They, too, headed to the base.

The base alert status was raised as a precaution but for most base personnel it would be business as usual. The officials had to take a 'wait and see' approach.

After the last unsuccessful Turkish coup, which we had just been through, the military sponsor and their spouses were given a briefing for the families. Military personnel living off base were assigned a location on base to retreat to if the Base Commander should declare an emergency.

The Next Few Months

Thanksgiving and Christmas were quiet and seemed a little strange being that we were in a Muslim country. We sorely missed the Christian trappings—the lighted Christmas trees and season greetings from everyone you meet. We made the house as festive as we could inside but not outside. It helped our Christmas spirit to some degree.

We made it through the long and seemingly endless rainy season from December to Mid-February. We were thankful for our large covered porch where the children had a place to play out of the mud, which was everywhere.

Mia. CJ, Chase, Imp and Sondra.

When spring arrived and all the blossoms in our garden appeared, we were grateful for all the water and rich soil surrounding the Adana area. We would soon be able to enjoy the delightful abundance provided by this amazing soil.

Shortly, it would be summer and we would be off to more adventures, to climb more castles and swim in gorgeous blue-green waters. Life was good.

CJ Visited by a Bear in front of Adana House.

Chapter 6
Our Hell Begins

And Our Hell Begins

It was dawn and the baby awoke wanting her bottle. As I blearily moved into the kitchen to acquire sustenance for this hungry little mouth, I heard the sound of a car door close in front of the house.

This was an unusual sound especially so early in the morning. None of our Turkish neighbors would ever be able to afford a car so I knew it must be our car door. I knew for certain, we had locked the car doors. We had put duct tape over the little window that had been broken because we could not find a place to get it replaced.

As I peeped through the small window in the front door, I could see a man in what looked like a uniform sitting in the car. Someone was apparently trying to steal our car maybe for the second time.

I darted the few steps to our bedroom to wake Chase!

After laying Imp down in her crib, I handed her the bottle and hoped she would not wake her brother and sister down the hall or alert the man outside!

I shook Chase out of a deep sleep and tried to explain about the man outside.

Chase and I whispered as he pulled on his jeans and grabbed his unloaded rifle. We kept our guns unloaded because of the children. The ammo was locked in a chest. The guns were still at home due to the attempted coup that had just taken place a short time before.

We tried not to let the person outside know we were aware of his presence. Chase quietly slipped out the front door and eased close to the wide pillar that supported the top floor over our porch for protection.

It was clear the man was wearing some sort of uniform. Was he military or police?

Chase called out to him, "Dur, dur" and then called in English, "Get out of the car."

The man opened the car door as Chase walked down the first few steps of the porch. The man came out of the car holding a large handgun pointed directly at Chase and me!

By this time, I was already out of the front door by a few feet. I jammed myself up behind the wide porch pillar near the front door. With my back up against the pillar, I saw Chase check for my safety and dive over the cement wall of the steps.

Then in the next second, our son appeared at the door. He walked out on to the porch in full view. Neither Chase nor I had realized CJ was there...*Oh, my God!*

As a shot rang out from the man's gun, I ran the few steps to CJ, grabbed him, pulled him down on the floor behind the pillar and threw myself on top of him. I was praying that the next bullet would not somehow penetrate through me to him!

As we dove for the protection of the pillar, I heard the sickening sound of CJ's head clunk slightly, against the cement floor.

As the second shot rang out, I lay there; almost resigned to the thought I would be shot. I was praying CJ would be okay. I did not know what had happened to Chase whom I no longer had in sight.

The thought of: "*Who here in Turkey could take care of our children if Chase and I were to die?*" raced through my mind. Then I remembered thinking, of all the silly things, "*How embarrassing it will be to be found dead, here on the porch, in my nightgown.*"

All these thoughts flew by in a second.

I waited in silence for what seemed like an eternity for yet another cracking sound to come—but none did!

Next, Chase was standing over CJ and me. The uniformed man had disappeared.

All three of us were still alive and miraculously unharmed. Mia came out of the house, grabbed her brother and started to cry.

We, all four, walked shaking into the house.

Can you believe our little Imp had gone back to sleep in her crib in spite of all the noise? CJ was stoical about what had just happened for a child his age—scared but brave. Mia was a basket case. Chase and I were totally confused as to what had just transpired.

The man in our car had torn through the tape on the wing window which we had put on after the first time the car had been stolen.

Evidently, he had opened the passenger door then slid over to the driver's seat and started working on the ignition wires as before. We later found our large screwdriver from the glove compartment was missing. We could only speculate that the man may have been the one or ones who had stolen it before.

When Chase ran to me to see if we were okay, in his concern, he had left the gun at the bottom of the porch.

Once in the house, our first job was to reassure the children that everything would be okay.

We were beginning to feel as if we were caught up in some B-rated movie.

What To Do Next

We gathered our thoughts and settled the children. We gave them bananas and milk then got them busy with a puzzle. I changed my clothes and then we headed for our Landlord's front door. We rang the doorbell and waited for our Landlord to answer. They were already headed down their stairs to see what was happening.

Just then, one of our Turkish neighbors came in the gate since the shots had awakened them as well.

Chase and I went to greet them and relay what had transpired.

As our Landlord opened the door and we were talking with our neighbor, an open-bed truck rumbled into the drive. It contained several armed guards waving their rifles in the air.

They jumped out of the truck and ran toward Chase and me. They were yelling something about 'were we American' and 'did we live here'. It was all in broken English and we were not sure what they were saying. Not waiting for our answer, they drug us both off to the waiting truck.

They saw Chase's gun. One of the policemen grabbed it and started laughing, unmistakably pleased that he had a prize.

Two men grabbed Chase and put him into the front. The other two threw me into the back of the truck.

I was screaming for help, "Someone, somebody, stop them!"

Through some miracle, our Landlord and our neighbor were able to grab my arm and shoulder and jerked me off the truck as it passed by just inches from where they were standing.

Luckily, I had put jeans on. My jeans were torn from the wood or metal on the truck as our neighbor and Landlord grabbed my arm and pulled me out. I was bruised and a bit scratched, but all my body parts were still in place and thankfully not broken.

The armed men, thank God, did not turn around and come back for me. After all, we were in Turkey and I was a woman.

Our Landlord whisked me back into their house. I was thankful now that I was a woman and of little value in this country.

Our Landlord's wife headed for our house. She insisted I go upstairs with her husband while she took care of the children.

My mind could not seem to grasp what had just taken place. I had no idea what to do next or where to turn.

It must have taken me a good ten minutes to get my brain to cooperate.

All I could think of was, *"My Chase, where were they taking him? And why?"*

Our Landlord made some chamomile tea to help soothe my nerves and to help me stop shivering.

I used their telephone and tried to call Chase's Commanding Officer on base. He would know what to do. Right? Then, it dawned on me that it was Saturday. The base operator would not give me his home telephone number.

Next, I called the base Air Police. There was a sergeant on duty who answered the phone. I tried to explain what had happened and begged him for assistance.

The sergeant sympathized but explained, "This is out of my realm of authority being it is a civil situation." He suggested I call the JAG office and he gave me the telephone number. It was Saturday so there was no answer, of course.

Our Landlord and I spent the next few hours trying to locate someone who could help determine where they had taken Chase. He worked on the Turkish side and I worked on the base side but neither of us got any information.

We were losing precious time here. Each minute, each hour, that passed could be putting Chase further away and more at risk.

When that truck drove away with Chase as a captive, I felt as though part of my heart had been ripped out and had been dragged away with him!

Our Landlord and I had done all we could for today to try to get help for Chase. His wife cooked us dinner at their house. She was a marvelous cook who obviously knew we were in need of comfort food that night.

As we were sitting at their dinner table, I had an overwhelming sense of needing to get the hell out of there quickly. I was not sure where that feeling came from but it was very real!

Our Landlord and his wife were equally as leery for both our situation and their own. They insisted I go back to our area of the house, get what we needed, and go to the base.

I totally agreed.

It was getting eerie as it would soon be dark and still *no* word of Chase.

And Then the Crowd

As we threw a few belongings into small suitcases, I first began to hear voices and then shouting at the front of the house outside the wall. They were now yelling furiously about "American." I could not understand what they were yelling because my Turkish was still very limited.

I peeked out the little window in the front door. The crowd was busy rocking our car from side to side and pounding on the roof.

One did not need to speak the language to know their intent. I asked for advice from a higher power. "*Oh, God, now what do I do?*"

It was obvious—we had only minutes until the crowd would become bold enough to break through the front gate and, then next, our front door.

One fleeting thought I had was to grab my rifle to protect us. Quickly, I realized this was not a viable solution. I certainly could not hold off a crowd with as little ammunition as I had especially with having three young children.

Then, there was the realization that, by the way, we were in an anti-American country to boot and protecting ourselves with a gun, would not be the best option.

Access to the car was obviously no longer an option either. Our only avenue of escape was through a small opening near the back wall of the house.

We would need to leave behind the bags we had just packed.

However, I did grab the baby's blanket. She would have been more dangerous than the crowd outside without her Bankie come bedtime!

Cautiously, I opened one of the French doors in the living room, which was on the side of the house where the crowds could not see us. I prayed that no one had yet come through the gate and onto the porch. If so, we were assured to be caught.

We walked quickly and quietly down the few stairs, staying very close to the house until we reached the back wall some forty or so feet away.

I put Imp through the opening in the wall while holding onto her hand in case she started to run off. I barely managed to squeeze through myself and then pulled CJ and Mia through in turn.

As I pulled the last child through the opening, I glanced up to see my Landlord's wife with her hand by their window blowing us a kiss.

I could feel her heavy heart even from that distance, feel her motherly sense of concern for us, and feel her trepidation about our safety.

We kept as low as we could while we crept through the tall weeds in the field directly behind the house. We managed to stay out of the view of the crowd that had formed out front. As we crept, bent over, I held Imp very close to me and hoped she would not make a noise or draw attention and expose us all.

We headed for our American friend's house, Joe and Sue's, about one-quarter of a mile away across the open field. I prayed, *"Please let them be home."*

The children were frightened but they seemed to know that we all had to be brave for each other and for Dad. I cannot tell you how proud I was of them and how amazing they were. They were made of good stuff like their Dad.

By the time we reached our safe haven, my back was aching from crouching so low. Imp felt as though she weighed a hundred pounds.

It was a miracle that no one spotted the children and me crossing the field. We most assuredly would have been visible to anyone who happened to come around the corner of the house.

We finally made it through the field to an area where there were bushes and trees to hide our movement. We stopped for a moment to catch our breath and stand up straight.

One more block and we were on our friend's street. It was now dark.

Then, only two blocks to go!

Mercifully, no one was on the street at that moment to see or catch us.

I pounded on Sue and Joe's door hoping they would respond quickly if they were there. Praise God, Allah and all the Saints they were home.

Sue and Joe were shocked to see the children and me standing at their door after dark. They were even more shocked in the coming hour to hear what had taken place with Chase.

After I filled them in on all the details, the three of us agreed that it was neither a good idea for any of us to be out in public, nor would it be safe to drive to the base right now. They both insisted the children and I stay in their house for the night.

Joe immediately used their telephone to call the base. He finally got hold of someone in Chase's squadron who assured him he would, "Get right on the matter, first thing in the morning."

The officer of the day at the base felt as we did—that we should all stay put for the night at Joe and Sue's house.

In reality, this decision was a gamble. Was it really safer for us to stay in a house where the neighbors knew Americans lived? Or, was there more exposure for us to drive a vehicle with American military license plates for all to see?

Sue provided us with clothes to sleep in. She too had a toddler and so she had the basic essentials. We fed all the children and snuggled them down for the night.

It was hard for us adults to go about all the normal bedtime process and not start talking about the day's events in front of the children. We all worked on making CJ, Mia and Imp feel as secure as we could under the circumstances. The children did not need to be made any more frightened than they already were. That being said, it took them a while before they closed their eyes.

I felt that too often adults drew children into worrying about matters that were not for children. In this case, however, the children had been too much a part of the event not to worry and be afraid.

After the children were asleep, the three of us went into the kitchen to eat and discuss the events of this grave confusing day.

It was impossible for me to get food down that night but my old security blanket, a cup-o'-tea, provided me with some measure of temporary warmth and comfort. A hot cup of English tea with cream and sugar, of course, had long been my standby in trying times.

That night, I tried to sleep. I knew that my ability to think straight and to have a clear mind was important—I had to get some rest.

Sleep was difficult for many reasons. First, to start with, I could not get comfortable on Sue and Joe's short, narrow couch. Second, I was cold because we had put all the extra blankets on the children.

Sue had given me her chenille robe to use in place of a blanket. It felt warm and cozy for the parts of me it covered but, due to its length, I only had the option of either keeping the top or the bottom of me warm.

Do not get me wrong—I was deeply grateful for the children and me being away from our house and for the hospitality our friends were offering. However, in the case of Sue's chenille bathrobe gratitude was not a good substitute for warmth!

The night seemed to last forever. Minutes seemed like hours as I lay in the dark trying not to wake the sleeping household. I eased myself quietly over to the window to look out but there was no moon in the sky at all. I saw no movement as I sat in Sue's rocking chair and thought!

All my mind would do was to keep replaying the events of the day...If only there could be a stop button for one's thoughts.

All I wanted to do was scream aloud, *"Where is Chase and bring him back, you bastards! How dare you put my family through this? What had we done to these people except to start to love their country?"*

I went back and curled up in a ball on the couch. A huge wave of feeling terrified took hold of me and then, just plain, good old-fashioned anger.

Actually, I thought up many four-letter words that perhaps, had not been invented until that night. A sailor would have been proud of me. The nuns from my private Catholic girls' school were probably rolling over in their graves—especially Mother Superior!

Until that night, I do not think I had ever used the s__t word once in my whole life. I must say thinking up those newfound words certainly helped to relieve the tension.

In reality, I knew I had to defeat the scared little girl feeling inside of me. I had to call upon the 'bullheaded Sondra side' to pull me/us through whatever we had to face.

The only thing I could do for Chase right now was to keep our family safe.

In my mind, I knew that he was a military man—that he was strong and that he had a good head on his shoulders. In my woman's heart, I also knew he was made of flesh and blood and, therefore, he was vulnerable.

His heart would break if anything should happen to his family—his life.

Wherever he might be at this moment, I knew that any fears or desperation he might be feeling were more for the wellbeing of the children and me than for himself.

Finally, I succumbed to exhaustion and began to fall asleep just as the sun began to rise and the children started to awake. Children always have the best timing... don't you know?

Was He Still Alive?

As early as was reasonable, I tried to call our Landlord and his wife to see if they were okay and to ask if they had heard from Chase.

I was anxious to know if we had any of our belongings left in the house and if the car was still there and in what condition it was.

The children and I by now needed a change of clothes and they were worried about their "stuff."

I dialed their number but their phone just kept on ringing and ringing—there was no answer.

It was Sunday. We called the base again and still no

word of Chase. I had to choke back the panic that was starting to build inside me.

"*Was he even still alive? No, I could not, I must not, even think those thoughts.*"

Joe called another friend in base housing and got him out of bed. Joe arranged for us to move into the VIP quarter (actually a trailer on base) for a few days.

It was a huge relief to know that at least the children and I would be safe on base. At the same time, I felt as though I was abandoning Chase by being on *the safe side of the wire*, so to speak.

Joe Would Take the Children

We decided that Joe would take the children and secure them on base with one of his friends until I could get there. I had my own mission to accomplish before joining them.

It was the best plan I knew but, at this point, I hated the thought of letting the children out of my sight even for a minute. I had to trust that Joe would get them safely to the base.

Joe borrowed a Turkish friend's car so as not to draw attention that he was an American, just in case. We dressed the children and Joe in Turkish looking clothing and off they went.

The plan was that after Joe had driven the children to the base, he would return with two of his buddies and a pickup truck. We would all drive by the house to scout it out.

If and when we got to the house and it all looked quiet, we would go get the suitcases we had hurriedly packed. And, hopefully, we would be able to start our car and get the 'H out of Dodge'.

Joe's friends were not very happy about me going along with them back to the house. Nevertheless, I had to get some of our important papers and, believe it or not, none of the three guys could drive our car because it was a stick shift.

We were concerned for them as well because they had no authority off base. If they needed to protect themselves or me they could, quite possibly, wind up with Chase.

When we reached the house, our Landlords were gone but they had closed and locked the shutters on the house. They left a note on our dining room table with one yellow rose that was now wilted from the heat.

The short note said to "Go with Allah." The yellow rose was the yellow rose of friendship. Both the note and the rose were a comfort because I knew that they still cared. Sweet Dear, she had sprinkled the note with her homemade rose water she knew I loved so much.

I was relieved. At least I knew we still had their support and love and they had left on their own volition. I was sure they had gone to their summer home for "a visit".

The car had been ransacked and anything loose was missing including the radio. The exterior was scratched but otherwise the car was in running condition, I hoped!

We had been at the house almost ten minutes when another neighbor came knocking at the door. He told us to leave quickly and not come back. He said he feared for the "safety of all Americans in the coming days" and then he left.

We scooped up as many belongings as we could along with two boxes of important papers.

It was surprising that the house had not been ransacked like the car. Evidently, our Landlord had worked some kind of magic and persuaded the crowds to leave things alone. We will never really know how they managed to calm the crowd and convince them to leave without doing damage to their house as well.

For a few minutes, I frantically looked for the car keys that were hiding in Chase's uniform pocket. I twisted my long hair on top of my head and put on one of Chase's Turkish looking caps. I did not want to look like a woman driving a car.

We locked the front door and went quickly to the car. There was no sign that anyone had opened the hood of the car. I hoped the car would still run. When I turned the key, the starter made a grinding noise and quit. I crossed my fingers and tried again with the same result. The third time was the charm. Off we went.

The trip to the base was without incident. All the way there I could not help but try to make sense of what was going on. There did not seem to be another revolution or coup taking place so what was happening? What was yesterday all about? All I could think of was, *"Oh, God, please, where is my Chase?"*

As I drove through the checkpoint and onto the base, I finally felt like I could take a breath.

Base Quarters at Last

No sooner had we reached our assigned quarters and I had kissed and hugged the children and unloaded the car than I got a telephone call.

A Turkish source had confirmed that Chase had been located. He was alive! He was being held in one of the downtown police stations, but why was he being held and on what charges? The Turkish source either could not (or would not) disclose the information.

Base Quarters.

The base official was told that an American Air Force officer would be allowed to visit him that afternoon. Only one official could go and he would only be allowed ten, perhaps fifteen minutes, with Chase.

They said I was not allowed to go with them!

I could not bear the thought I would not be allowed to see him, to hold him, to comfort him, and to share with him all of the ordeals of the last thirty-plus hours.

I was furious because I was not convinced this was true or if the base authorities were just saying that to prevent me from going.

When the base official arrived at the police station, Chase was nowhere to be found. The Turkish police "had to move him to another police station," so they said. The Turkish Policeman conveniently did not know to which police station he had been moved!

We were not to locate him until two long days later!

I Made Enemies

That evening, our first evening on base, the children and I were invited to one of the officer's houses for dinner. Two other officers and their wives were invited as well.

They fed the children early. By 7:30 p.m., when dinner was served to the adults, I was worn out but the food was delicious and I had not eaten but very little in two days.

Be assured, I deeply appreciated the effort his wife had put forth.

I tried to be polite and listen to the women chitchat about what was to me, at that moment, such superficial prattle. They were trying to take my mind off what was going on and, for their courtesy, I was appreciative but we so needed to be able to go back to our quarters.

I needed to be alone with the children. I had to get a bath and some rest. The children and I had not had alone time since this had happened and we desperately wanted "*it*"—our time alone. They needed, I needed, to be able to get a bath and to read them a bedtime story. We all craved at least a few hours of a seemingly normal family routine.

It was crucial to assure the children that God would keep their daddy safe; that he had done nothing wrong; that they could be proud of their dad!

As soon as I felt it was the proper time, I started to thank our hostess and say my goodbyes to the other women.

As I got up from the chair, our hostess grasped my arm firmly as though I was a kindergartener who had just 'done a no-no'. I was startled as she forced me to sit back down and then apprised me of what their husbands had decided.

The children were to be farmed out each to a different household for as long as it was going to take. She said it had been decided that it was too much for anyone to handle three children and all that was going on— especially for such a young girl like me.

Shock set in from her demands.

I felt that fight or flight instinct kick in about two seconds later. It was all I could do not to scream at them.

I wanted to say, "*It's well and good if you want to play the weak female. I cannot play that role.*"

I could not afford the luxury right then of saying what I really thought, so I did not.

I wanted to say, "*This is the bullheaded Sondra you are addressing. You obviously have no idea whose daughter you are talking to!*"

But, I squashed the thought and instead I told them I appreciated the offer to help but there was no way the children and I were being separated.

I did my best to bow, scrape, act appreciative and at the same time be equally as firm about the fact that our children were staying with me.

Enemies were made that night. I never received one offer of help with the children from that day forward—at least not from them. I cannot say I blame them. I was not my normal sweet self. I was worried to death, tired and needed a bath. Most of all I needed alone time with my children. They needed to be tucked into bed by their Mother, not some stranger.

It became obvious later that God really guided me that night. Had I allowed the children to get out of my care it would have been ammunition for *Him* (an unnamed base official) later on. *He* would have turned it around and said I had fallen apart and they had to take care of the children.

They (some and/or one of the base officials) later were to become the enemy. *They* were the ones who in the next few weeks and months wanted me to go back home. *They* wanted me out of their hair; wanted me to shut up; and assured me they would handle everything. *They* said, "they would take care of Chase."

He would try to justify sending me home since *He*

claimed it was too much for one young girl to handle. *He* would say that the children and I "would be better off back in the states."

Let me explain my referring to They/He. I will not use real names and in some instances, I never knew who they were. They were whoever was trying to hush this event. They were the officials (here or somewhere else) who were trying to make my voice go away.

I assure you that I knew who *He* was.

Chapter 7
Anti-American Feelings

Our Turkish friend who had taken us to Heaven and Hell heard about our plight. He got word to me about where Chase was located. I was not quite sure how he located either Chase or me. It only proved this was a mysterious country with silent eyes watching around each corner—even on a secured base.

Damn the Turkish police! He was still in the same police station where he was originally taken!

I called the base legal department. Capt. Mack would be the officer in charge of this case. He called someone, who called someone, who called someone else. Capt. Mack went to the station within the hour.

When Capt. Mack arrived at the police station, he found that Chase had been beaten but not where it would show. He was weak and obviously already had a fever. Capt. Mack spent about twenty minutes with Chase. He took him a change of clothes, a note from me and the children, and some military rations.

Capt. Mack reassured me Chase was holding up in spite of all he was going through.

I did not hold much credence with his report about Chase's health. I knew he would say that even if Chase were not doing well.

Most of all Capt. Mack said Chase was worried about the children and me. Capt. Mack said he was very relieved to find we were okay and safe on the base.

I could tell from Capt. Mack's face that he was concerned about Chase's health despite his reassurances from before. He still had no idea about what was going on.

There were still no official charges on the books. Chase was being held on "Pending charges" but charges for what?

It was obvious Capt. Mack was somewhat at a loss about what to do next. Due to the Status of Forces Agreement, an American Military Lawyer had no authority in this country.

The Status of Forces Agreement

The Status of Forces Agreement was signed and put into effect on June 23, 1954, in Ankara, Turkey. It is basically an agreement the U.S. makes with a foreign country in order to rent their property and put in an airplane patch and some buildings. In exchange for the privilege of renting a piece of their turf we, the U.S., give that country copious amounts of money.

The small print in the agreement states that all American military personnel no longer have any rights as American citizens off base should the Turkish government determine they have offended any laws of that country.

There is more to this agreement but the reason we need bases in Turkey is to give the U.S. closer access to countries like Russia and the rest of the Middle East, but you get the picture.

As I was not a part of the original negotiations of the Turkish/American Status of Forces Agreement, I had no right to question the capabilities or motives of the people involved.

However, I cannot help but surmise that perhaps they should have selected a mother who had experience in negotiating a truce between two two-year-olds! If they had, perhaps, we would have come out with a more equitable agreement.

In my humble opinion, it was obvious that on the day of this agreement there had been a higher level of Turkish testosterone in the room than American!

Back to Chase

I could hardly bear to think of what Chase had been going through. I only wished I could comfort him and care for him.

When Capt. Mack had been allowed to visit him for those few minutes, he had been able to give him the clothes, our short notes and a few aspirins that he had in his briefcase

The next day a Turkish lawyer assigned to the base, recommended trying to get Chase moved to the prison instead of the local police station.

Since Chase was a foreigner, the Turkish lawyer felt there was a good possibility of making this happen. They would try to have him moved into the political prisoner section. There, the Turkish lawyer said, he should be safe from any more beatings.

The local police were known for their extreme cruelty from what we had heard.

Someone, somewhere, worked a miracle. Chase was transported to the prison the next day.

It was surreal that I should be relieved that my husband was now being moved, to a prison!

The base officials would not let me go visit him during the first few days Chase was in the prison. Capt. Mack, the Turkish lawyer, and our friend Joe (an M.D.) went to see Chase.

Joe was able to examine Chase and give him medication for the phenomena he now had contracted. He gave him medication to help his busted eardrum and found Chase had two broken ribs to tape up before he left.

Capt. Mack came by the trailer to give me the details of their visit. He asked me to just call him "Mack" from now on. So, "Mack" he was from that day forth.

For obvious reasons, I did not tell the children about their Dad's condition.

Anti-American Feelings

Subsequently, we learned there had been articles in the front page of the Turkish paper and on the Turkish radio about the "Mad Dog American" trying to shoot a local Bekci. (Bekci translates to private security guard.)

All I could think of was, "Where the heck did that come from? Chase's gun was not even loaded. No one was hurt! And, certainly not that idiot who shot at us!"

It had been the radio report that had brought the crowds to the house within the hour after the news had aired late 'that afternoon.'

All the publicity about the Mad Dog American was to stir up more of the anti-American undercurrent that was being promoted by the Turkish Government.

Within three days, two other American military men had also been arrested. They were all to be used as leverage by the Turks.

One GI arrested was a young man who was driving

with his family for a short outing and had a dead baby thrown in front of their car. This was not an uncommon occurrence. Usually, it was a lamb or chicken or prized rooster.

With an animal, the driver had to pay on the spot for having just killed the family's only means of making a living in order to avoid not being stoned. I was told that normally the fine to the driver was based on the amount of money he had in his wallet at the time.

The Turkish girl baby had obviously been dead for several days, they said.

The young GI who was driving with his wife and two small children barely escaped being stoned by the mob even though the police were already on site.

The family was all in their car when the crowd appeared. One man who pretended to be sobbing from the loss of his child demanded the money. The couple was pulled out of the car as some of the Turkish people started to pick up stones.

The police who were watching the whole scene, at long last, intervened. The police told the crowd that they were in charge and instructed the crowd to go home.

The police shouted at the young woman to get back into the car and to drive away or they would arrest her, too. That act in itself was strange as women usually did not drive in Turkey and how did they even know she could drive?

She returned to the car and drove off as fast as she could, knowing that as a woman in Turkey, she should not be driving at all.

As she drove down the road, she could see in her rearview mirror that her husband was being pulled toward the police car.

The next day, after her husband had been arrested, the Turkish authorities showed up at her house and confiscated their car.

Whether these specific incidents were planned or whether the government just gave the order to take advantage of the next few opportunities to acquire hostages, who knows. The Turkish government definitely wanted these Americans for future leverage to use in their Cyprus cause.

In retrospect, it certainly gave me the impression that the choreography worked too well for this not to have been planned in both cases. The police always seemed to be as though they were standing by in both these incidents. In Turkey, there was no 911 to call, so how did they respond so quickly if they had not been forewarned?

I Finally Got to See Chase

On the next day, I was informed that I could go to see Chase if I wanted. I was warned that it might be a bit sensitive for me. Our incident had been plastered all over the newspaper again about the Mad Dog American being transferred to the prison.

I wondered, "*What exactly did they mean by sensitive for me?*"

Mack and a young Airman from my husband's unit picked me up in an officially marked Air Force vehicle.

On the way to the prison, we drove past a small village with a few people going about their daily business. The people in the village gave our American military vehicle little notice—all seemed calm.

As we neared the prison, about a dozen angry Turkish people started to run toward the car. It was now clear that they had been waiting for us to arrive.

Our driver drove up as close to the front gate as he could which was about fifty feet away.

The prison, as you would expect, was a large, dirty, old ominous looking cement structure.

As Mack and I got out of the car, the villagers started to yell and throw stones at us.

One of the prison guards standing by the door watched the whole scene unfold and did nothing to help us. Another guard took mercy and let us in the door to safety. We evidently zigged and zagged when we should have because we were not hit by even one small rock.

I decided that if I ever have to move to another Middle Eastern country that it should only have sand—not rocks!

Mack and I were hoping that Chase would not find out what had just happened as we entered the building because it would just make him worry more. If he knew, he probably would not let me come to the prison again.

Mack waited outside the official's office where Chase was to be brought to me.

I could not believe this was happening. I could not believe that I was waiting there in a prison to see my husband.

Less than two weeks ago, we were the All-American family, enjoying newfound friends and barbecues. We were playing on the beach and swimming in those warm blue-green waters.

The door opened and there was my love. I started to hug him but he pulled back. He hurt too much to let me touch him. We kissed and held hands. He did not want to let go and neither did I.

He shared with me a few details of what had happened to him in jail. I could tell it was still much too painful both physically and mentally, to share all there was to tell—at least right now.

I told him briefly about our journey since that awful morning. I, like Chase, withheld the gory details of us having to escape from the house through the field because of the crowd. I did not mention the first night on base and how they tried to separate our children from each other and from me.

We were each trying to protect the other.

I assured him I would be there every day until he was safely home with us. I could tell he was very grateful. Chase was stoic outside but I knew him and I had the sense that part of him was feeling scared and abandoned inside.

About that time, Mack came in and explained the little he knew of what was officially going on.

As Mack started to say something about the SOB Turkish police, I got a feeling that we were not alone in the room.

Cautiously, I walked around the room. There, on the side of the desk, was taped an old microphone with duct tape no less. I pointed to the side of the desk and made a gesture for Mack to hush.

The cord on the microphone ran into a desk drawer on the other side. They had obviously never watched 007 movies or they would have been more astute. More aptly, whoever installed this apparatus must have been Clouseau's dumb cousin from The Pink Panther movie.

From that time on whenever Chase and I wanted to share information we did not want the Turkish authorities to know, we walked in the hallway and whispered in each other's ear as we pretended to hug.

The hugging part was good. If only it could have been 'sweet nothings' that we were whispering instead of plans to save our lives.

About Turkish Prisons

Allow me to explain about Turkish prisons. Little, if any, food was provided to the prisoners except for a little rice. Either a prisoner needed to have someone bring them food and other life necessities; or they shared with the other prisoners; the other prisoners shared with them...*or they died.*

I cooked Chase a hot meal every day to take with me when I went to visit. I always put in something for everyone to share. He also had his military rations, for back up, if he should need them.

In the political prisoners' section of the prison where he was now, there were about a dozen other men. What a variety of ethnicities they were. I might add in this prison, there were less than one-hundred total number of prisoners.

Chase was the only American and the only military man. Most of these swashbucklers had been caught running drugs or guns or other contraband. One man had been imprisoned for whistling at a police officer's daughter.

Most were well educated, interesting and apparently seemingly quite reasonable people, according to Chase.

They all lived in a big open room with cots and a place to cook Turkish style over a charcoal fire.

The sanitation was terrible with no hot water and no heat in the winter. With the incessant hot temperatures being what they were, there was no way to get cool in the summer.

Then, there were the other tenants—the bugs and rats.

The men in his section all looked out for each other. They especially felt indignant over the Turkish government's arrest of Chase as a military hostage.

There was no love lost between his roommates and the Turks by any means. One man was of Greek descent and two were Kurds. None was of Turkish blood.

They seemed to take the Turks bad treatment of Chase personally. He was now their friend!

The highlight of the day for the roommates became the chance to see me, and later the children and me, come to visit Chase.

When Chase got back to their dorm, they all wanted to hear every detail of what the children and I were doing for that day and the next.

It became their connection to home and family in some small way.

The Days Dragged On

For the next few days, I dodged the rocks going from the car to the front door of the prison. I became rather proficient, if I do say so. My gym teacher in school would have been proud.

Gratefully, the number of people waiting for us at the prison started to dwindle in the following days.

A week or so into our visitation trips, I was notified the base would no longer provide me with an escort or transportation to the prison.

My heart sank. As a female, it would be very dangerous to drive our car to the prison each day.

By now, the local Turks knew what I looked like. With the U.S. Special Forces plates on our car, it would not take any time before both the car and I would be easily recognized.

The cost of a cab would be out of the question. Taking a bus with three children and food for Chase would almost be impossible.

Yet another hurdle to jump, "How on earth was I going to get there each day?

As I walked into Chase's CO's office, he could tell I was upset and at a loss. Bless his heart that wonderful man came up with a solution.

From here on out, until Chase was released, each day an ambulance was to take us from the hospital to the prison, in spite of what I had been told. Chase's Commander's attitude was that the ambulances were under his command and so was the budget to provide the fuel. By the way, the driver was always a volunteer and on their off-duty time.

It was interesting that from the first day I started to arrive in the ambulance, there was never another stone thrown.

From the second day on, there was no one outside the prison that bothered us. Thankfully, this was one problem solved.

I could perhaps take a breath and no longer worry about what would happen on my way into the prison the following day. I could perchance get a little more sleep.

Moving Again

That same day, when I returned to the VIP trailer, I had a message to call Chase's commanding officer. He had arranged for our furniture to be moved out of the house downtown and into base housing. He said someone would come to pick up the key to the house downtown in a few minutes, if I was available.

It was obvious that it was unsafe for the children or me to go back downtown to Adana to live.

The following afternoon I was given the keys to our new quarters. It was an old German-built trailer with a wooden addition on the side. The addition consisted of a small living room and an even smaller bedroom. But, at least, it was on a secure base.

About two o'clock, two large trucks stopped in front of our quarters with all our belongings. Several of the men in Chase's squadron who were not on duty had volunteered to pack and move our household goods.

I was exceedingly grateful to these men even though their talents were obviously not in packing and moving... however, I did not have the heart to suggest they might need to keep their day jobs!

The price was right! They would not even let me buy them pizza or a beer. A couple of them offered to help unpack but, by that time, I did not even know where to start. Things were piled everywhere.

Our new home/trailer on base was ironically next door to the trailer that Gary Powers, the U-2 pilot, and his wife had lived in before his famous and disastrous flight over Russia.

There were a few slight problems with our place. The utilities were not hooked up and we had no electricity or gas. We did have water.

No power meant no lights, no refrigerator, and, worst of all, no air conditioning.

There was no way to give the children a hot meal, unless, of course, I would have cooked it on the pavement out front. I was considering it because the temperature was one hundred and fifteen degrees outside the trailer near the pavement one afternoon.

The nights were miserable, as well. It was usually long after midnight before it was cool enough to fall asleep.

I took the children to the commissary and BX to cool off most days before we went to visit Dad. We went to do our shopping—so everyone thought!

Each day I would call to see when someone was going to hook up the utilities. Each day it was the same old song, "Maybe tomorrow."

By the sixth day, I had had it.

I searched through our packed boxes and found the cutest outfits that Imp and I possessed.

If I couldn't get someone's sympathy, I was certain that Imp, our adorable nymphet could...*Sometimes one has to use the resources at hand!*

With absolute determination and dressed for action, we drove to the airplane maintenance hangar straight away.

There were several Airmen working on one of the planes. I called out, "Is there someone here who really knows their stuff on electric and propane gas?" They looked at me rather strangely.

That was a set up on my part because each said he was the very best, as they each raised their eyebrow and grinned. We all laughed!

"OK, gentlemen, decide who of you is really the best," I said.

They all pointed to one tall lanky guy.

"You," I said while trying to be charming. I pointed to the young man they had chosen. "Follow me, please. This is an emergency and we need your help!" To which Imp added her adorable little girl "Peas", to seal the deal.

"Please bring the tools you need to hook up electrical and propane gas," I requested.

As my grandma would have said, he looked a little befuddled.

He grabbed some tools and got in a pickup and, hallelujah, he followed us to the trailer.

That afternoon we had electricity and gas all thanks to that tall lanky man. I could not help but hug him, to which, his face turned bright red.

Visitors

The day after we had moved into our new quarters, I had visitors. I was somewhat embarrassed as I scarcely had a place for them to sit with all the boxes.

Most were wives I barely knew and some I had never met. They had only come to get all the gory details of what had happened. They, of course, said, "We'll be here for you."

We never heard from them again, as they had acquired the gossip for which they had come.

In all fairness, I realize that it was much too hot for them in two aspects. Physically, in the non-air conditioned trailer as well as politically. One never knows where the chips might fall. It would not do to align one's self with someone whose husband was in prison... now would it!

Later, I would ask everyone I knew to write to his or her Congressman to try to get support for Chase. Not one of the women who came at first to get the scoop and offer help would stick out their necks when we finally asked.

It is understandable to some extent. It would not have been good for their husbands' careers. It would not be good for a career military person to be making waves with his or her Congressman nor for his or her spouse to do so either. It was against the unwritten rules.

I wanted to believe there were a few that would have liked to help and did not dare.

The Children Visit Dad

After three days of no rocks and no angry Turks, I felt that it was safe to take the children to the prison. They desperately needed to see their Dad and him to see them.

It was important for them to be as much a part of his life as possible under the circumstances, both to support their Dad and to make him realize he was still their all-time hero in their eyes.

Our three children were in desperate need of their Daddy's hugs and he of theirs.

Chapter 8
Clotheslines and Messages

On the same day that Mack returned from his three-day leave in Lebanon, he came to tell me that word was out—I was going to be forced to go back to the States.

They wanted me out of the way. "*They* would take care of my husband," he had been told.

Now I understood, that this was the reason the utilities had not been turned on. I surmised *They* were under the assumption that if things were uncomfortable enough I would certainly pack my bags and 'want to go home'. *They* did not know my mother's daughter. *They* did not know that I would not leave this country without my love.

As one of our children's books said, "I would not, should not, and could not leave."

Charges are Brought

Mack's voice hesitated for a second as he told me that there had been charges brought against Chase. Mack would soon be officially notified what the charges now were.

This was, of course, no surprise to us. It was obvious that the Turks intended to use Chase for their political benefit.

By this time, it would be a relief, in one sense, to know exactly what we were facing. Being in limbo was excruciatingly hard on all of our nerves.

The next day our children were invited to a birthday party. I insisted that they should go to the party instead of going to the prison. The woman who invited them was the only neighbor who was willing to help us. Thankfully she insisted that I leave Imp too so that Chase and I could have a few minutes alone together.

Our friend Joe (also a Doctor) decided he would be the one to escort me to the prison that day. He was still worried about Chase's eardrum—it was not healing well and his phenomena were still lingering.

Joe examined him; gave him some pills and medication for his ear; and left us to spend a few precious minutes alone. Chase seemed unusually disheartened. My heart ached for him because he was feeling guilty for putting us through this. I thought to myself, "*As if you have a choice, my love!*"

When I got back to Joe's car, we sat and talked for about fifteen minutes. Joe was a good friend of ours by now. I could trust him with my feelings or so I thought.

I asked Joe what, in his medical opinion, we could expect. Would Chase still be the same mentally when this was over?

I started quietly to cry. I was not hysterical but I just needed to let a few feelings escape through the valve. After all, Joe was a friend...right?

An Official Visit

That same afternoon, the Base Official summoned Mack and me to his office a few hours after I had returned from my daily visit.

There were three of *Them* plus Mack and me. We introduced ourselves politely. *They* made small chitchat about how cute our children were and how brave I had been.

Their patronizing attitude toward me was disgusting.

They talked about how getting Chase out of prison was of the utmost importance to them. *They* were going to have someone go down to the prison several times a week to see Chase, take him food and give him support. Well, if not several times a week, at least once a week. *They* would make sure that the doctor checked him at least once a month.

I immediately thought to myself, "Wait a moment! It unquestionably seems from that statement that *They* feel he is going to be there a long time."

"Excuse me, Sirs, it seems as though you have some knowledge that my husband is going to be in prison for a long-term type of deal. Am I reading you correctly?" I questioned.

Annoyed, *He* dismissed the others in the room by saying, "I would like to talk with Sondra for a few minutes alone...now."

Realizing that *He* was, shall we say displeased, Mack and the others exited the room as fast as they could without stumbling over each other.

The minute the door closed the conversation went like this:

"Young lady, I know you have your husband's interest at heart. A young girl like you can't be expected to understand these complicated matters. This is a man's business to handle," *He* said smugly.

"Young lady, if I was in the same situation, I know my wife could not deal with this and I don't expect you to either. If I were in your husband's shoes, I would not want my wife around; I would send her home. It would be much better for your husband if you took the children and went back to be close to all your family."

"Sir, I'm sorry about your rapport with your wife but my husband and I have a very special relationship between the children and us. We need to stay together. If the situation were reversed, I certainly would not want my husband to go and leave me. Have you asked him how he feels about the subject?" I asked.

"Young Lady, I know as a man, he would want you to go home," he said with disdain.

Determined, I stated, "Sir, with all respect to everyone, I will not leave this county until my husband walks out with me. I have sent letters asking for help from Congressman Ed Gurney."

Then, he informed me of what he had been doing. "I am certain that when you wrote those letters you were not thinking straight and you were too upset. I have taken care of all that for you—to save you embarrassment."

He handed me the letter I had mailed to Congressman Ed Gurney a week or so before along with the other four I had mailed about the same time.

Then he said that Capt. Joe Denton told him I was hysterical today after our visit to the prison. Joe had said I really lost it.

I was crushed! Joe—our friend, right! I was furious with myself for having let my hair down, so to speak, with Joe.

He then went on to say, "My dear, we can't have a hysterical girl to deal with, too. You will do no good for your husband. I am recommending that you *decide* to go back to your family in the States."

I will have to admit that I lost my cool. I probably should not have said what came out of my mouth next. It tipped my hand.

"Sir," I said, "I will tell this story to every television station, newspaper or anyone on the street back home that will listen. I will not be silenced. If someone does not make a commitment to get my husband out of prison and safely back home, I will shout it from the rooftops. Sir, I will not let his/our situation be brushed under some, not so magic carpet."

"Honey, now calm down and be realistic. All you would do is muddy up the waters. I think you better re-think your attitude and leave strategy to those who know what they are doing, that is, if you really care about your husband. Besides, Honey, there is more involved here than just your husband," *He* gruffly spouted.

I then dared to question him, "Sir, I am asking you to level with me. What is really going on diplomatically between the U.S. and Turkey? Something serious is or has happened and we are caught up in its tentacles. We have the right to know."

He refused to say another word on the subject! *He* knew or thought he knew that I had no resources for acquiring much information. How wrong he was.

It was obvious that our situation was not his priority. I did understand that there was more to this situation than just Chase. I wanted to say, "You idiot! I have traveled and lived in many parts of the world and, by the way, my degree is in International Relations and Diplomacy! I got it!"

He told me that our meeting was over and to think seriously about what he had said to me.

"Okay, Sir, I will think about what you have just said. Thank you for your candor."

I was not lying. I would definitely be thinking about what he said and I did appreciate the information.

Now I knew what really was going on behind the scenes with *Him,* at least. I knew how I had to start playing the game.

This meant that I would have to go underground, so to speak, with my activities.

I would bite my tongue and pretend to play along or so He would think!

My Strategy was Clear

When *He* had handed me back those envelopes, the ones I had already mailed, I knew that *He* had silently declared war.

Obviously, any mail that I sent was not being allowed to get off the base.

A picture seemed to be forming in my crystal ball: the view was now vividly clear why my telephone calls were never getting through to the U.S.—presumably because of the heavy static.

"Okay, so what's the plan here?" I said to myself as I drove back to quarters.

At that moment, I was too mad to think of any plan. The only soothing thought at that specific time was of my hands placed tightly around *His* neck. The idea of castration was a delightful thought to me.

Then, I said to myself, *"Okay, so I will say a few extra Hail Mary's for my previous thoughts."*

From that day on, I knew I dared not share my scared feelings with anyone on base. I never knew when they might be used against me.

Instead of sharing my feelings, in the quiet of the night, I would pretend Chase was there to hold me. I cried in my pillow at night and prayed it would all go away.

I worried about how I could care for three young children on my own in these threatening times. I wondered if I could stay strong enough... I felt so alone.

From that day on, I knew that I was fighting on three fronts at the same time. It was the old triangle! *Ah, yes, little grasshopper, there were many angles to consider.*

The three fronts were as follows:

• *Him/Them* (A few military officials, representing our government who wanted to hush up this incident)

• The survival of my husband and our family unit

• Turkish Government

In school, Chase and I had been on debate teams; had run in competition; and were both on swim teams. We now had the hardest competition of our lives ahead. We were swimming upstream against the current.

"Please, GOD, Please, we desperately need help!"

Chase was Not to Know

Just as I had not told him about most of the, shall we call them, adversities that the children and I had been going through since that awful morning, I did not tell Chase that *They* were trying to send me home. He had enough worries already.

The next day, however, I did ask him if he would prefer that the children and I go home. He clearly was hurt and somewhat taken aback by my even mentioning such a possibility. I assured him that I should not, could not, and would not go without him.

That night the children and I ate dinner and played a few silly games and they laughed. We laughed.

It was good to hear them being happy and carefree. It was good to be silly. They had been so brave, so loyal and I was so proud. There had been too much heavy stuff in all our lives since that day. We all, assuredly, needed this welcome respite.

The Phone Off Base

The next morning, I asked our neighbor if she would watch the children and she said she would.

I decided to take a chance and drive downtown to our old house to use the phone. I muddied up the back of the car to hopefully disguise our U. S. Forces license plate. I hoped our Landlord would be at home. If not, I would go to our Turkish friend's house to use their phone to make a call to the States.

Our old house downtown still had the shutters closed. I was disappointed. How I would love to have been able to see them both if only for a few minutes.

I drove past the house and then on to our other Turkish friend's.

I felt relief, when I saw they were home.

At first, they did not recognize me. I had dressed as much like a boy as I could. They welcomed me warmly; told me to hide the car in their front gated area (where it would not be seen); and ushered me into their study.

They insisted that I have tea while I told them as many details as I could. After we were finished, they left me alone to have privacy when I made my call to Steve.

Chase and I had a dear friend in the States named Steve Demopolis. Steve was like a brother to the both of us. Steve, age thirty-five, was a paraplegic but he was undoubtedly one of the most amazing, dynamic men I have ever known. All of us gals back home agreed that Steven definitely had that Greek charisma!

Steve had somewhat adopted our children as he had no children of his own. He had been paralyzed while playing college football and then sadly his new wife left him shortly thereafter.

Steve would always tease Chase. He told Chase on more than one occasion that he was trying to find a way of getting him out of the picture so he could have the children and me. They used to have fun teasing each other and me. These two were so simpatico that I used to kid them and tell them to "Go get a room."

Steve also was a good friend of Ed Gurney who was our Congressman from Florida. I had been very active in Florida during Ed's election as well.

Two of the letters that *He* had returned to me yesterday had been the ones that I had sent to Steve. In those letters, I explained our plight to Steve and asked him to please call, Ed.

I had not considered the time zone difference when I made the call. Steve was home but I had awakened him out of a deep sleep. He could hardly believe what I was telling him and he was in a state of shock over the news. Steve said he would call Ed as soon as he possibly could!

He told me to get back to the base and stay there! He said he would send his mother over to Turkey to get the children and take them back with her if I needed.

Steve knew that I would certainly not let anyone but his family take the children. The children all loved them as family and they would have felt safe and very much at home. Besides, Steve's Mom was a world-class Greek cook and the children loved her food!

Steve knew that sending the children back to my mother was not an option for several reasons—not that she did not love them or would not try to be a good caregiver.

I told him we were okay and were hanging in there. He sent Chase his love and we ended the call.

After hanging up the phone, I felt a bit of relief. At least now, we would not be fighting this alone. We were now, connected to an ally!

I was comforted with the knowledge that if I needed to get the children out of Turkey there was a place for me to send them.

That comfort was short lived when I realized the passport situation. Because Imp was on my passport, she could only travel with me!

I tried to imagine what the odds were of me getting two new passports issued so that I could stay here in Turkey and then send Imp and the other two children home to the States in an emergency.

Our Turkish Friends

Our Turkish friends had been trying to help us as well. They were still working to find out what were the official charges against Chase. They too wanted to know what was going on behind the scenes with the Turkish authorities concerning Cyprus.

They did find out Chase was not the only man being held which, of course, we already knew.

They were equally sure it had to do with the situation in Cyprus. They were certain that these men would be used for leverage to persuade the Americans to support Turkey in their problems with Cyprus. America had thus far refused.

This was not what I wanted to hear, needless to say, but the pieces were starting to fall into place.

Our friends and I arranged to meet in the little village outside the base in two days. It would be safer for me than driving to town.

Clotheslines and Messages

They told me that one of their maids could get onto the base and she could pass on any message to me. She would tuck the message in the end of our clothesline and I would do the same. She would check each day and so would I.

In the next couple of days, someone had meticulously made two endcaps and placed them on one side of the clothesline. Now neither passersby nor the children could see any messages left at the end of the clothesline.

We soon changed our clothesline code. If one of us left a message we put one single clothespin on the right side of the line. One clothespin meant it was ok to wait 'til dark to retrieve the note, two pins meant to retrieve it as soon as possible.

A History Lesson on Cyprus

During our next meeting in the village, our friend said he felt it was necessary for us to understand the history between Turkey, Cyprus, and the U.S. He said if we did not know their history, we could not fully understand what we were facing.

He then tried to condense the recent history for me...

Cyprus and Greece were under British protection for many years.

The makeup of the population in Cyprus was mostly

Turkish and Greek Citizens.

Cyprus became an independent country in 1960 after a bilateral agreement from both Turkey and Greece. The Treaty of Alliance established that Greece, Turkey and Britain would assure the integrity and independence of Cyprus. Tripartite headquarters were established by both Turkish and Greek military in Cyprus.

The Treaty of Guarantee designated the same three countries: Greece, Turkey and Great Britain to guarantee Cyprus independence.

As British world power declined, the U. S. replaced Britain in the role to support the two other countries. The U. S. Congress and public were against the move. However, the threat of the USSR (or Communists) taking over of Cyprus, Greece and Turkey forced the U.S. to step in.

The treaty provided both Turkey and Greece equipment, etcetera, to assure the independence of Cyprus. However, as both countries were now members of NATO, they must abide by NATO's rules and subsequently NATO must approve of the arms and equipment.

Our friend said that this boiled down to the fact that there was constant fighting going on in Cyprus between the Greek communist factors and the Turks. He had heard rumors that Turkey intended to invade Cyprus but the United States, as one of the NATO leaders, would not partner with them. The U.S. was concerned about getting involved in a war with the USSR over Turkey—in a lesser territory.

My head was swimming with all his information but it did clarify the Turkish attitude toward the United States. Our friend told me that there were upcoming Turkish elections, which added to the upheaval as well.

Now we knew that this was not just a general Turkish dislike of Americans, but it was a serious political agenda.

I totally had a headache by the time I got back to quarters from trying to absorb all the details.

The Guardian Angels

The next morning our guardian Angel came disguised as a man. He drove up and got out of an Air Force vehicle. "*What now?*" ran through my mind.

It was Sam, our neighbor, who lived downtown. He and his wife had a son that played with our son occasionally. Sam came in and I offered him some coffee but he said he did not have time.

He said he had to talk quickly.

Sam and his wife turned out to be our two Guardian Angels sent from heaven to help in any way they could. They felt so strongly about helping us that he was willing to jeopardize his military career, if necessary.

I prayed, "*Oh, please, let me know if I can really trust him.*"

He was attached to a unit that knew everything that went on at the base. He actually knew what was going on even before *He* did.

Sam said that this would probably be the only time that he would come to our quarters but he would get word to me when he needed. He would help guide us—meaning Chase, Mack and me—as much as he could.

He even offered their home if we were ever to have to move back downtown for as long as we needed.

Sam said *He* had sent a message requesting orders for the children and me to be sent home. The request was to be given "Top Priority."

There was another request—one that concerned Chase's pay and allowances. Chase's pay was to be stopped due to the fact that Chase was no longer able to report to work or able to perform his duties!

He also said Chase had been arrested on a civilian matter not military-duty related and that justified his pay to be stopped.

When those two requests came across his desk, Sam had chosen our side—he was pissed off.

I did not tell Sam about our Turkish friends, just in case. If he did not know who was helping us on the Turkish side then he could never let it slip. I could not compromise my sources.

Nor did I tell Mack about either Sam or our Turkish friends—at least not their names. I just gave him the information as it was given to me.

I hated to be so untrusting. It was not in my nature but, for all our sake, I did not dare take a chance of totally trusting anyone except Steve. It would be too easy for someone to slip in an unguarded moment...too easy to let precious information slip, information that could, perhaps, compromise our position somewhere, sometime.

Chapter 9
The Hearing Day

Bugs

Mack came by a few minutes before our daily trip to the prison. It was strange. I let him in the front door and he immediately put his finger to his mouth as if to say hush and then he motioned for me to come out of the trailer.

Once outside he quietly told me that he had uncovered the fact that the trailer had been bugged. There was one microphone in the kitchen and one in the telephone, which was also in the kitchen. The listening devices had been installed three days earlier when I had been at the prison.

When asked, the neighbor told me there had been a utility truck in front of the house while I was gone...*Darn*.

I was infuriated that someone had invaded our privacy and embarrassed to think that someone may have been listening to our conversations. I had nothing to be concerned about but it was just the idea of being listened to and watched that galled me.

Thank heavens that Mack had found out about the bugs.

Although I was certain it was illegal to bug our place, what was my alternative? I had to go on about business as usual at least for now. In turn, I made Sam aware of the bugs as soon as I could.

After that, when Mack and I were strategizing, we drove to the flight line and took a walk. Mack made the comment one day that sooner or later someone would start the rumor that there was something going on between the two of us if we were seen together out of his office... *Oh, well!*

A Bit of Good News

Finally, a month after Chase had been taken hostage; Mack had some good news to share or at least some progress to report. Chase would go before the Turkish judge in three more days.

Mack said the 'powers that be' seemed to feel that there was a chance that the Turkish/U.S./Cyprus situation was ebbing or perchance had blown over. They felt hopeful that 'our situation' could be over the day Chase went before the judge. They were reasonably sure the Turks would release Chase.

I could not believe that Chase might be home in a few days. We might soon have our lives back once again. I could hardly wait to see him and give him the news if he had not heard already!

We had a mini-celebration at our visit that afternoon. I stopped by the commissary and bought cupcakes and ice cream for everyone...we were so excited.

When I arrived back home after our visit there were still moving boxes stacked up everywhere. I had not had any time to deal with much more than putting the basics away. I hoped we would not be staying in Turkey very long after Chase's release so no need to put it all away. I assumed they would transfer him to another base or back to the States immediately.

I could not let Chase come home to a mess like this. I worked all night, most of the next day and into the following night to make sure everything was just right.

I could hardly move from lifting so many heavy boxes and pulling furniture around.

Part of the reason for all the work was for Chase's arrival. The other part, frankly, was because I had to keep busy—to keep my mind off what might be. I was excited and apprehensive and I had to burn off nervous energy.

The Second Night

The second night I finally quit working around 2:00 a.m. I was exhausted. I decided to call it quits. I turned off the light, went to bed and quickly fell asleep.

Within a very short time, something woke me up. There were noises at the bedroom door. It sounded as though someone was trying to pry open the door or jimmy the lock.

My mind was racing as fast as my heart—had some Turk somehow gotten on the base to harm us or to set up another incident? Was this perhaps another plot by *Him* to scare me off?

Still sleepy and too exhausted to be thinking straight, I was having trouble focusing on what was actually happening.

I got up and headed toward the door which was only feet away from the bed.

Suddenly, I absolutely froze. I literally could not move for what seemed like minutes while I weighed what might be happening.

My mind was racing. What would happen if I had to

protect the children and myself? Legally what would another incident do to us? Could I, too, wind up in Turkish jail even though we were living on base if it involved a Turkish citizen?

I caught a glimpse of the doorknob turning.

Any second now, I would be facing someone with perhaps a gun or knife in hand and I could not even move!

Then, silence, no more noise or movement at the door.

It seemed like an eternity before I regained my ability to move, I slumped down on the bed and turned on the light. I was shaking so much when I went to the kitchen to call the Air Police that I could hardly dial the phone. The policeman on duty halfheartedly took the report over the phone. I think he thought that I had either lost my mind or was drunk.

That night I saw headlights from the police car as they patrolled periodically through the night. I was grateful!

There was no way I was able to fall asleep the rest of the night.

I located Chase's old soft terrycloth robe with its lingering scent of his after-shave cologne and wrapped it full around me for protection until dawn.

Sunrise could not come soon enough.

I absolutely could not fathom why I was so frightened or that I reacted as I did.

The worst part of all was it made me doubt my own responses. I had not reacted like that on *that morning* or at any other time—so why that night?

Had I become 'gun-shy' so to speak?

In a sense, the gun-shy factor was true. For months, I was startled by any loud noise and so was CJ. After *that morning,* CJ no longer wanted to play any games that involved shooting guns!

I made a note to myself to buy four dead-bolt locks the next day—one for the top and bottom of each door just in case!

From then on, I would leave the outside lights on even though I hated to sleep with bright lights coming through the thin window shades.

Off Base Became Off-Limits to Me

In the morning, there was a note in the clothesline with two pins attached to the line. It was from our Turkish friend. It read, "*Please to meet me this afternoon to 1:00 p.m. in usual place.*"

By noon, I was headed to the village.

I rode my bike to the front gate of the base as if I were out for exercise.

I had to leave the bike at the bike rack near the checkpoint, as I knew better than to try to ride a bike off base.

As I started to walk past the checkpoint, the Airman came out from the guardhouse. "Nice day, isn't it? Not as hot as usual. I'm going into the village to buy some Turkish bread. My children love it. See you later," I said.

As I continued on my way, the Airman startled me when he asked me to stop and show him my ID.

They had never asked for ID to get off base. They check coming on the base, yes, but never going off!

When I showed him my military ID, he looked at the name and told me I could not go off base. The guard said that the orders were that "I was not to go off base unless officially escorted."

"*Son of a gun*! *Those were the orders left at the gate for the guards by Him.*"

There was nothing for me to do but turn around and ride back to our quarters. I was furious and feeling very trapped.

Not being able to meet our friend was a huge worry. What intelligence might he have gathered that he wanted to discuss? What information did he have about tomorrow that we would now not know?

As soon as I returned to quarter, I left a note of apology in the clothesline to our friend and a brief explanation of why I did not make our meeting.

We were to have met in the village in the back garden of his friend's business. I knew where the business was but not its name.

Even if he actually did have a telephone, I could not have called from our bugged phone.

The Hearing Day Begins

I dressed in the most conservative Turkish style clothes that I could find. I put on a dark navy-blue long skirt; white long-sleeve loose-fitting blouse; a long-sleeved blue jacket that almost matched; and flat shoes.

I knew that I would melt from the heat. But, this was the dress code and it was appropriate for the occasion. I did not want to do anything that would irritate the judge or make Chase look bad in Turkish eyes. Yes, I would put on a scarf just before I went into the courtroom.

Mack came by to take me to the courthouse. He approved of my choice of dress. Mack wore a gray civilian suit.

At the courthouse, in a small dimly lit hallway, several

Air Force officers joined us. The Turkish lawyer, procured for Chase, arrived shortly thereafter. By law, Mack could not represent Chase in the Turkish court.

The Turkish lawyer ushered Mack into another room halfway down the hallway from where we were standing. Then, the Air Force officers and Turkish lawyer spent about fifteen minutes talking with Mack before it was time to start the court proceedings.

Fifteen minutes hardly seemed enough time for a lawyer to know much about a case. Mack said that to his knowledge the Turkish lawyer had not had any contact with anyone from the base regarding Chase's case before he walked into the court today.

We all proceeded to the courtroom where the case was to be heard.

The room was large with towering ceilings. It almost reminded me of a church instead of a courtroom. It had long wooden bench seats just like a church. The judge's platform was raised like an altar and had a huge old plank-like table from which the judge would preside.

The Turkish lawyer told Mack and me to sit on the left side of the right section in the second row of seats. We were not to sit too close to where Chase would be seated. Chase would be seated on the right side of the first row.

He asked the other men to be seated in the back. He was annoyed with them for having worn their military uniforms off the base, which was normally against military rules.

Mack and I took our seats. There were a few people already in the room—sixteen men to be exact. I wondered who they were and why they were here. They were not all sitting together but scattered here and there. They appeared to be businessmen. They were not dressed as peasants by any means.

Mack surmised that one group might have been from the consulate. If they were from our American consulate, I would have thought they would have come over to say something to us.

We had all been seated about twenty minutes when the judge and his little entourage came in the door. The judge slowly walked over and sat rigidly in his seat. He was a large harsh-looking man, larger than the average Turk.

Shortly thereafter, the double doors in the back of the room were thrown open and in came the guards with Chase.

Chase was flanked by four local Turkish police—not the prison guards. They had rifles in their hands and bandoleers full of bullets. Their presence and their attitudes were, to say the least, intimidating. Terrifying would be a better description. They were there to make a statement!

Even more of a concern for me was that Chase was once again at the mercy of the local police.

As Chase came closer to us, we saw he was in handcuffs. They did not do this at the prison. I wanted to scream at them! How could they degrade him this way?

My hands were down beside me on the bench. I clenched my fingers so tightly out of anger that I broke the skin on my hand from my fingernails. My hand was bleeding. I did not realize it until a few minutes later when I felt something warm and wet.

Not wanting to get blood on my skirt and not having any tissue with me, I rubbed the blood off my hand onto their bench. I asked Mack to scoot over. When Mack realized my hand was bleeding he gave me a handkerchief from his pocket.

Chase tried to look around to see if he could locate us

but one of the policemen started to hit him in the chest with his rifle.

The judge called out for the policeman to "Dur effendum" in a rather harsh voice. *Dur effendum* meant "stop friend" in Turkish. The policeman looked embarrassed for having been chastised in front of everyone.

The judge's assistant then called the court to order.

Let's Get This Over

I could only hope that: "*Now, perhaps, we could finally get this ordeal over and done with and get Chase out of here today. All we want to do is put this in our past and get on with our lives.*"

Deep down, I knew that this was not going to happen—at least not now. If their intent was to let Chase go then why were they treating him so roughly? It did not make sense that they were still obviously flaunting the fact that they were the ones in control.

The hearing was over in only a few minutes. The judge motioned for Chase's Turkish lawyer to come forward and then the judge mumbled something we could not hear.

The lawyer walked back to Chase's side and said, "Sorry." The judge then raised his hand to dismiss everyone. The guards quickly herded Chase out of the court not even allowing him to talk to his lawyer or to us. Mack and I stood there with our mouths hanging open.

As Chase went by his face was white.

I turned to Mack in bewilderment; his face looked almost as blank and white as Chase's face had looked as he passed by. Mack and I walked over to the Turkish lawyer. As we started to talk to him, the other Air Force officers came over to find out what had just taken place. What was the verdict?

The judge had told the Turkish lawyer that Chase was being held on the possession of a firearm and the discharge of a firearm which had resulted in an injury. He, the judge, would have to decide if these charges would actually be brought against Chase by the next court date.

The next court date would take place in maybe three months. "No release for the American" was the judge's predetermined verdict.

One of the Air Force officers said, "Hell, they can't keep on doing this. It's not legal." Mack turned to him and said, "We're in Turkey or have you forgotten? We are playing by Turkish rules now—whatever those rules may be!"

You could tell Mack was gut mad not only as a lawyer but also as an American citizen.

After Chase was taken out of the room, we spoke briefly with the Turkish lawyer. He said the judge's attitude was one of "America is going to be taught a lesson." The lesson was not just meant for us, personally, but for America. The lesson was to make America realize that Turkey was in control.

I asked the Turkish lawyer about the injury charge. To what injury were they referring? We were the ones that had been shot at for heaven's sake! It was true, however, that Chase held a gun beside him even though it was unloaded. He had not had time to load it. Remember, the police had grabbed it that fatal day when they took Chase.

"What are we to expect now?" I asked. The Turkish lawyer's response was, "Be patient. Our system works on slower time and with different introspection than your American ways."

He excused himself and took his leave.

Thoughts Turn to Chase

Our thoughts quickly turned back to Chase's safety.

We had so many questions in our minds... Would the police take him back to the prison? Would they play hide and seek with him yet another time? Was their intent to beat him for the second time, in some out of the way police station, given their newfound opportunity?

We drove back to the base followed by the Air Force officers in another car.

On the trip back, Mack and I did not utter a sound. Mack had no answers. He was at a loss for words..."*You know it's bad when a lawyer can find no words.*"

Back at our quarters, I changed out of my dreadfully hot sticky clothes and cleaned off my bloody hand.

Next, I tried calling Steve even though I knew the phone was tapped. Our telephone line would not connect, as usual, for a long distance call. Of course, I had no luck getting my call through to the States. I dare not try to call from any other phone on base.

Mack soon came to the trailer and we had a glass of iced tea and a sandwich. He called the base officials in spite of the static on our phone. He wanted to see if they knew of Chase's whereabouts. They knew less than we did at this point.

Mack and I decided to drive to the prison. We were anticipating that by this time Chase should be there if, in fact, that was where they had taken him.

We did not take the children. They were at the neighbor's and I called her to tell her we had important business to attend to the rest of the afternoon. She told me to take my time.

Back to Prison

We drove again in silence through the streets to the prison. We were both apprehensive that Chase might not be there when we arrived!

Heartbroken myself, I questioned: *"How was I going to tell the children that Daddy would not be home tonight?"*

I prayed, *"Please God, at least, let Chase be back at the prison unharmed."*

We went into the front hall of the prison as we normally did. The only thing they would tell us was, "To wait."

The attitude of the guards seemed different. We sat on the narrow bench waiting for almost an hour. Our nerves were getting frayed.

Mack and I had not thought to bring a bottle of water in our rush to get to the prison and we were getting thirsty. Certainly, we did not want to ask for water knowing of its disgusting source if they took it out of the faucet.

Finally, they brought Chase through the door. He looked so drawn and dejected.

During our time with Chase, the three of us were extraordinarily subdued. Chase and I just sat and held hands. Neither of us spoke. We did not have to. We could feel what the other was feeling; knew what the other was thinking. And, it was not good.

We were appreciative that Mack did not add insult to injury by trying to give us false words of hope.

While we were there, surprisingly, Chase's Turkish lawyer came by the prison to talk with him. I might add that this was the first time that he had shown up to consult with Chase.

The lawyer had confirmation of what we had feared

was true. Chase and the other two men were being held as hostages to use against the U.S. as leverage concerning the Cyprus situation.

Our Turkish friends had told us from the start that they suspected this was the case and they were correct.

He apologized for his abruptness in court. He said he did not want the court authorities to view him as being friendly with the American. He said he had more advantage if they felt he was more on the Turkish side.

The Turkish lawyer tried to prepare us for a very long haul in our quest for Chase's freedom. He said his people were not about to budge. He was very sorry about his country's ways. Next he asked Mack what the American authority's position was on the Turkey/Cyprus problem.

Mack could not answer because he really did not know. The officials were not sharing much information with Mack—perhaps they themselves did not know for sure. If in fact they had a position, Mack was not privy to the information.

They did not want to admit that these men were being held hostage over the Cyprus state of affairs. *They* certainly did not want the news media back home to get wind of this story. *They* wanted to pretend that these three men were involved in totally separate civilian incidents. *They* wanted to sweep these incidents under the carpet for political reasons!

It appeared that if Chase were to be held in prison for the rest of his life, it would be "just one of those things" to *Them*. Chase could easily become expendable.

I now realized how critical it really was for me to stay and be Chase's eyes and ears and most importantly his voice.

It was harder than usual to say good-bye to him as we

walked out of the prison that afternoon.

This day had brought such disappointment for us both. The reality that it would be a long, long road to gain his freedom had slapped us in the face!

A Day of Disappointment

It was dreadful having to tell the children that "Daddy would not be home tonight." They were so, so disappointed.

I fibbed a bit and told them that the court date had been postponed.

It was getting harder and harder to keep the true seriousness of the situation from Mia and CJ.

That night when I was putting the children to bed and reading their bedtime story, the words all seemed to blur and all I could see was their daddy's face on every page.

With the children all tucked in and my cup of tea in hand, hoping to relax a bit, I suddenly remembered my missed appointment with our Turkish friend.

Had he had news about how this day would evolve? Had he been trying to lessen the shock perhaps?

My concern now was, "*will I forever be restricted to the base unless I am officially escorted out the gate?*" If so, it would certainly make my communication with the outside world almost impossible.

Thank heavens I had the mailbox—the clothesline. It might turn out to be my only line of communication.

That clothesline used to be a place that I would prefer to avoid and now it was my friend.

Chapter 10
A Stranger on the Road

The next day was our anniversary and it was heartbreaking. At least we were still all alive. And, where there's life, there's hope or so they say. We should not, would not, could not, give up.

We tried to make our anniversary a little festive. I baked a huge cake for all Chase's roommates to share and I took ice cream in a cooler. Chase and his roommates and the guards were quite pleased. It was a huge treat for all of them.

The children made Happy Anniversary signs and gave them to Chase along with a few balloons. He said it would certainly help brighten up 'the dorm' as we referred to his living quarters.

Chase seemed in somewhat better spirits when we left.

Our Present From Him

We were to be given quite an anniversary present. The present came from *Him.*

When I got back to quarters after our visit with Chase, Sam was waiting for me. I was surprised that he had actually come by our quarters in broad daylight... You know his rule.

Not knowing if our conversations in the kitchen were still being monitored, he motioned me to come outside to talk.

The word had just come in that the children and I were to be sent home within the next few days! He had to warn me. He said he would be back as soon as he had any more news and we would work out a plan.

Sam was right. I was summoned again to *the office* within the hour. I already knew about the messages *He* had sent thanks to good old Sam.

Once in the office, *He* said, "Honey, I just wanted to tell you in person what has been decided. You and the children can no longer stay on base. You are no longer authorized base housing since your husband is not officially on active duty. Arrangements are being made to send you and your children back to the states—probably within the week."

"Oh, and by the way, Honey," *He* said, "your husband's pay will be cut off as he is not officially able to perform his duties!"

He seemed to take great delight in the fact that *He* had the upper hand, at last. Obviously, in his little mind, *He* was convinced I had no choice but to bend to his will.

"How do I put it, Sir," I said, "I am not leaving this country without my husband. If I have to move off base then I guess I will. I may have to send the children back to friends in the States for their safety but I will not leave."

"You see, Sir, *someone* does not seem to understand. I have money to last me at least ten years on the Turkish economy."

I probably should not have but then I said, "And, another thing, Sir—the children and I actually like Turkish food."

He snapped back, "Now, young lady! You do realize this will be placing both yourself and your precious children at risk!"

I politely retorted, "Sir, if this were your family would this same thing be happening to them?"

He did not say a word.

He started getting up out of his big leather chair as if to say, "Our meeting has concluded."

His face was turning beet-red probably as much from embarrassment as from anger.

"Thank you, Sir," I politely said. "I appreciate your time. But, I have to get back to the children and get in touch with any news media that will listen to our story."

I turned around and with a determined voice excused myself and then I left.

I Had Some Money

My father had died when I was twelve and I had a small inheritance. There was equity in our house and a few stocks that I had bought with the inheritance—thank goodness.

Given a little time, I could accumulate about thirty-five thousand dollars by selling them all.

I will give you some comparison of the cost of living in Turkey at the time. The average Turkish wage was thirty dollars per month and Chase's salary was about five hundred and thirty-two dollars per month plus allowances. Our house payment in the States was one hundred and fifty-eight dollars a month for a nineteen hundred square foot house in a nice neighborhood. The hundred and fifty-eight dollars a month was a stretch for us with three children so we lived on a very strict budget.

My threat to *Him* was genuine. I was staying in Turkey with Chase but my mind and heart were racing. In reality, I was terrified of the prospect of having to move myself and the children back downtown—even with our friends.

I would be endangering our friends, as well as my family, if I did. I knew there would be repercussions from the Air Force against Sam and his wife if we were to stay with them.

Subsequently, Sam's anonymity and delivery of critical information to us would be lost.

The thought of being separated from the children made me panicky. I knew that Steve and his parents would love and care for them but how could I possibly live without our children, even for a little time?

What would the effect be on these little people? Would they think I loved their daddy more than them?

If we were to be forced to move back downtown it would only be a question of time (in this reasonably small town) before everyone found out where we lived.

I, the wife of the "Mad Dog American" as the papers were portraying Chase, would be in danger.

How could I possibly put the children at risk? How could I possibly do without them if I were to have to send them back to Steve and his parents?

I could not abandon their father, not for his sake, not for my sake, and not for the children's sake either.

If I were to need to send the children back to Steve, logistically how could I possibly get them back to the States? An adult would have to travel with them. It would have to be me because Imp was on my passport.

There was no question that if I were to leave the country even long enough to fly the children home, the

Turks would never let me legally come back across their border.

How would I be able to get back into Turkey? I would not even know the first thing of how or where to illegally cross the border.

I was reasonably sure that U.S. officials would immediately seize my passport the minute I stepped back on U.S. soil.

Even if I could sneak back into Turkey, I would surely be arrested as soon as I was found. Then, what good would I be to Chase?

Our family was a unit; we had to keep that unit in one piece no matter what.

"How, dear Lord, do I solve this?

"Please, you do the miracles and I'll do the legwork.

"Right now, I can't possibly bring myself to think about making any of these choices.

"None are options. Please, God, don't make me have to choose between them!"

We were all doing our part to keep us going... Chase, in his way, by showing courage and keeping up his spirit every day. I, in mine, by being 'Bullheaded Sondra.' And the children, in theirs, by being good and loyal to their dad.

Another Trip to Call

Assured that I would be stopped again at the main gate if I tried to leave without being officially escorted, Mack granted my request to drive me downtown.

When we arrived downtown, I purposely did not let Mack see where I was going or tell him what I was up to.

He dropped me off and went to a little outdoor café to drink Turkish coffee and read while he waited. I was to meet him back at the café within an hour or two.

I deliberately went the opposite way and then around the corner and walked the few blocks to our Turkish friend's house.

I needed to use the phone to call Steve back in the U.S. I was concerned as to how long it might be before the Turkish government started monitoring all calls to the U.S.

The thought ran through my mind that I somewhat doubted they even had the technical capability to monitor calls unless they knew the exact telephone number in question.

Since I had only used my friend's telephone once before to call Steve, hopefully it was not enough to alert the officials.

When I got to their house, they were not home. Their maid recognized me and let me in immediately. I told her I needed to use the telephone and she ushered me toward their study!

My fingers were shaking when I dialed Steve's number and prayed that he would answer. "Hello, this is Steve, may I help you?" "Steve this is Sondra." I started talking a mile a minute.

I wanted to blurt out all the information to him before we were disconnected. I told him in one breath about Chase and the new charges; that the children and I were going to be kicked off base; and about Chase's pay and allowances being cut off.

Steve made me slow down.

"The heck they will, baby," Steve said. "You cry it out right now then go back, hug Chase for me when you see him, kiss the kids for me, and let me take care of that son of a gun."

I started bawling like a baby as I blabbered on...*At least I knew it was safe to do so with Steve.*

'Sondra, if I have to get my entire family over from Greece and send them to Turkey, I will. I'm getting pissed off at those Turks for messing with my friends. It's time to bring out the big guns!" he said.

"Now remember...do just as I say, baby, and in this order," Steve said, "Hug Chase and kiss the kids. Don't get it mixed up because this Greek don't kiss no jailbird." He laughed.

I started laughing and crying at the same time. He certainly lightened the moment.

Steve told me to hang up...because he had calls to make. He promised we would be in touch soon.

The phone clicked. Steve had hung up. He had calls to make.

Winston and Teddy

Winston Churchill and Teddy Roosevelt had long been my heroes because of their resolve about many facets of their private and public lives.

Teddy's statement about speaking softly and carrying a big stick had rather stuck in my small pea brain since I was a child. I doubt that I actually knew what they meant at that age but it stuck in my memory.

It probably seems strange for a teenage girl but I had read everything I could get my hands on about Churchill. When I was in high school, I was fascinated with his WWII experiences and then somewhat disappointed when I read his WWI history.

The first time I went to Europe with my mother was in 1950. The aftermath of the war was still apparent in some places where we traveled. For example, there were still a few bombed out buildings in London that had not been rebuilt.

Tales of England, especially during the war, had a genuine fascination for me!

In view of the fact that I was only sixteen when I started college, I was too young to join in with my older classmates in their after-school activities, so I read a lot.

One particular statement from Churchill stuck in my mind, "An English bull dog's nose is short in order that he could firmly clamp his teeth onto something and still breathe without letting go."

I now rather relate as I am mostly English, my nose is rather short and I have been called bullheaded. I just have to learn to breathe and not let go.

So, I had a little one-way conversation in my head with Teddy. "*Teddy, I have been trying to use your speak softly and carry a big stick theory. I have been speaking softly as much as I can. I only wish I could find a bigger stick; mine seems rather small right now.*"

Four days later Teddy's BIG STICK was handed to me right in my very own kitchen... *Perchance, was Teddy's spirit listening to me the other day?*

We Kept on Visiting

In the meantime, the children and I went, as usual, to see Chase each day. We heard no more about us moving— at least so far.

I kept waiting each day, hoping not to have to start packing. Of course, the problem of packing paled against the potential of having to make the decision about the children.

Mia went with us most of the time to visit her dad. CJ, now almost six, insisted on going every day no matter what. Mia needed to do every day normal things some days and did not go. It was understandable; she was, for heaven sakes, only seven and a half years old.

Imp, now two plus, had to see daddy every day. Besides, the way I looked at it, Chase might have been in prison but that was no excuse for him to get out of sharing, his little darling.

It was 'his little darling' that was already starting to get into the TT stage (Terrible Two's).

Actually, it was good for Chase to be involved in some part of our everyday lives. It was an immeasurable help to me as well. I did not feel quite so alone when I was able to share part of our daily lives with Chase. That is at least until I walked out the front door of that damned prison.

A Stranger on the Road

One day, as we were on the way to the commissary, I saw a young and obviously American girl with two small children sitting by the side of the road.

As I got closer, I could tell she was crying. It seemed strange there was no car anywhere in sight.

I pulled our car over, got out and asked her if I could help in some way. "Is your car broken down? Do you need a ride to someplace on base?" I asked.

She was sobbing so hard, I could not understand a thing she was trying to say.

Not realizing she could have taken a shuttle bus, she had tried to walk from the gate to the headquarters. She gave up when one wheel broke on the stroller she was pushing. The children with her were her one and two-year-old daughters.

As her story started to unfold, I discovered that her husband was a young, Army enlisted man. The Turks had arrested him. They, the Turkish authorities, had confiscated their car so she had no transportation. Even if she did still have their car, she as a woman, should not be driving in Turkey anyway.

She had taken a local Turkish bus to our base and was dropped off at the base's front gate. She was trying to get to some place on base where she could find help. She had no idea of where to go.

In order to give myself time to think of how to help her, I invited her back to our quarters. As soon as I got back, I hoped that I could get to the bottom of what was happening to her and her children.

She willingly took me up on my invitation.

To make a long story short, her husband was one of the other men who had been arrested.

They had been the ones that had had a dead baby thrown in front of their car. They had been the ones who had barely escaped being stoned by the mob.

The last she knew was that her husband was being held in a small village about forty miles away. She had no idea what to do next.

They lived off base and now she had no car. Her money had run out a few days ago and she could not seem to get any base official to give her help... *She had come to the right place*!

First, I fed them and sent her and the children in to get hot baths while I found them all clean clothes. I had to go see Chase shortly so I invited her to stay until I got back and told her to make herself at home.

That afternoon when I returned and we had a chance to chat. She breathed a big sigh of relief when I told her they were welcome to stay the night—we would make room.

She was obviously grateful.

That night we got all five children snuggled down; put on our pajamas; curled up on the couch; sipped on big cups of spiced tea and ate cookies, which always makes things seem better.

We talked for several hours. It was good to have someone who actually could relate to how I felt and to relate to what we were going through. I was careful not to tell her about my hidden sources of help.

We shared our ordeals of the past few weeks. I let her know about her husband's rights. He was entitled to be provided with food, medical care, and legal services from the base personnel. I clued her in about the system.

She fell asleep as we talked. She was feeling safe and comfortable for the first time in a while.

I gently woke her up and led her to my bedroom. She mumbled something about, "Oh, I could not take your bed."

I insisted she would sleep on the bed and I would sleep on the couch. She understandably needed a good night's rest.

The next morning we had breakfast while our children played a short while with her two little ones. I gave her most of the money I had from my purse which was about fifty-five dollars. I knew she was desperate.

After all, the children and I had enough groceries to last for a while. At least Chase's pay had not been cut off, yet. Fortuitously, I did have access to money when and if I could sell the stocks and get it in my hands.

If it became necessary, I knew I could borrow money to exist from Steve.

I told her where I thought she had to go to get her husband's pay. Her husband was in another branch so I was not as up to date on all their regulations. Poor dear, she was a brand new military wife.

She came from some place in the South. She had never been out of the town where she was born until she came to Turkey...*talk about a double whammy.*

We sent her on the bus with a bag full of groceries.

I never heard from her after that day which made me concerned for her—for them. We never knew exactly what happened to her husband either.

That night, I put a letter on the clothesline for our Turkish friends.

There were several favors to ask of them. Could they be of any help to this young woman and her husband? Would they please telephone Steve in the U.S. and see why I had not heard from him or Ed Gurney, or somebody. Finally, could they please inform Steve about this other couple?

In the following days, my friends reported to me via the clothesline that they could get no answer at her front door. It was not long they said until a moving truck came to pick up their household goods. They assumed it was for shipment back to the States.

Mack told me later that her husband was still being held and there had been no attempt to move him to the prison as far as he could find out.

One can only assume some officials had gotten to her and convinced her to go home.

Knowing full well the desperation and sadness that she must have felt, my heart truly ached for her.

Chapter 11
Two Big Sticks

Not One but Two Big Sticks Arrived

Sam broke his own rule for the second time. He came to our quarters, knocked, and then came right in and tossed two pieces of paper on the table—both were copies of telegrams.

Now, mind you...Sam was a very quiet, efficient, controlled sort of man. After he tossed the papers on the kitchen table, he started to do a little Indian War Dance around the table. He did not speak...the 'bugs' you know.

I could not stop laughing. It was a crazy sight. I wondered just what he had been smoking!

Watching his cavorting almost made me forget about the papers on the table.

When I started to read them, I could hardly believe it: TWO big sticks!

The first stick—a telegram from General Curtis Lemay. That read:

"To: Base Command, Incirlik Air Force Base, Turkey. Stop.

"Under NO circumstances will the pay and allowances be stopped for the men recently arrested by the Turks. Stop. Under NO circumstances shall their dependents be ordered to return to the U.S. unless they so request. Stop. If dependents would normally be authorized base housing, all attempts to relocate them to base quarters or continue their presence on base quarters, will be accomplished. Stop. All military personnel imprisoned will be provided with every possible service that we can provide, irrespective of what the Turkish Government normally allows. Stop. I personally, along with my staff, will be monitoring the passage of events in these matters. Stop. Military nor their dependents are not to be denied private communication via mail or any other means of communication. Stop. General Curtis Lemay. Stop."

The second stick was a telegram from the Office of Congressman Edward Gurney. It read:

"Dear Sondra,

"Have been contacted by Steve Demopoulos. Utterly shocked to hear about the events of your husband's imprisonment and of the ordeal you and your family are enduring. Stop. Understand that your husband is not the only U.S. military man to be in the same situation at present time. Stop. I apologize for not being there to assist you sooner. My office had no idea this had transpired. Stop. Be assured, Sondra, my office will be on this matter from here on out. I have contacted General Curtis Lemay. Stop. Please be aware, however, there are political differences that are being factored into this situation. Unfortunately, your husband and family seem to have been caught in the middle. Stop. I personally will do all possible to put pressure where we need it, but this is a very delicate situation in the diplomatic world these days. If it were in my hands, this matter would be ended today, but it is not. Stop. In light of the problems you have had in the last few weeks in communicating with anyone in the CONUS, if either my office or Steve has not heard from you at least every four days, someone from my office will contact you or know the reason why. Stop. A message to the base authorities from General Lemay should clear up any confusion the base authorities may have, as to the support you and your husband are to be provided. Stop. My direct telephone number is 555-555-5555 you may call collect, at any time. Stop. Sincerely, Congressman, Edward Gurney. Stop."

I was ecstatic...I did a slightly different dance than Sam had performed. I did the t-w-i-s-t.

I was flying high at that moment. I could almost imagine the look on *His* face—*He* who was so determined to get me out of Turkey. *He,* who did not want anyone to know about these 'incidents.'

Yes, there is a God and God knew I needed a big stick!

Until that point, it seemed all I was doing was walking backward. Now perhaps, we could start to move forward, if only in slow motion.

Most importantly, I would not have to choose between being with the children or their dad. We had a long way to go but at least our situation was stable for the moment.

This news also meant that we were not going to have to do without our American Ho Hos from the commissary after all...*there are priorities.*

Sam motioned that he had to go and then headed toward the door. I put my hand to my heart to say "Thank You." We did not speak a word.

We Had to Tell Chase

I could not wait one more moment to tell Chase. I called the Airman who usually drove us and asked him if we could go a little early.

I fixed Chase a sandwich, some potato salad and some cookies. That would have to do him for today. I woke Imp up from her nap, changed my clothes, and we headed out of the gate.

When Chase came out of his dorm, he was at first concerned that I was there so early. "Is something wrong" were the first words out of his mouth.

"On the contrary, my love, I have great news," I blurted out. His eyes lit up with anticipation of the news I was about to share with him.

At first, there was disappointment on his face as I unfolded the story of how *He* had been trying to force us off the base and how *He* was trying to cut off his pay.

Chase was, to say the least, extremely pissed off. After all, what had he ever done for his country but risk his life to protect our flag?

I could not understand his lack of excitement over my news at first. Then, I realized he must have thought that my excitement was over news of his release.

How stupid could I be!

Reaching down into my bag, I pulled out the copies of our TWO BIG STICKS and handed them to him to read.

Based on what I told Chase about us potentially being thrown off the base and his pay and allowances being discontinued, he quickly realized the importance of my news.

We were thankful for the BIG STICKS that had been delivered to us today. We now had something to give us hope on at least one front.

That Night We Partied

Back in quarters that night, I told the children that we had two messages offering us assistance and concern. They were impressed with the names on the pages. They felt most important that night!

We celebrated with a box of Ho Hos (their favorite) and glasses of milk with a little coffee at their request. They felt quite grown-up having the two messages and coffee!

The coffee in the milk was just a little fun thing Chase did with the children sometimes. He would sneak a wee bit of coffee into their glasses supposedly behind Mom's back. I always pretended not to see. Then, Chase would wink at me and I would wink back.

I was feeling guilty that I had not thought to take Chase some, too. In my excitement to tell him about the Big Sticks, I had forgotten.

Tomorrow, I would buy an entire box just for him.

Chase and I Were Close

Chase and I were very close—closer than most couples I knew. We had both grown up only children and raised by one parent.

Chase's mother had died when he was born. When I was very young, my birth father, a B-24 pilot, was killed when his plane was shot down off the Burma coast in WWII, killing all the crew on board. My adoptive father died when I was twelve.

So family, commitment and building our own family traditions for our children and their future children to enjoy were truly important to us.

It may seem trite, but Chase and I got a kick out of all the stages the children went through—well most of them anyway. We savored many moments with them that some parents might take for granted.

As a family, we loved to camp and swim. Soccer was our game.

We wanted the children to participate in all the usual activities: Brownies, Cub Scouts, Judo and ballet lessons—whatever their choices were to be.

It may seem old-fashioned, but Chase and I tried to teach the children to stop and smell the roses not only in the garden but also in life.

It had been additionally hard in many ways for Chase and me since he had been imprisoned. We were used to sharing our thoughts and experiences of the day. I did not feel completely whole without him in my everyday life.

When Chase and I were together for prison visitation, we usually had the children there so our personal discussions were somewhat limited. Sometimes we could coax the children to visit in the prison courtyard or have them play a game outside the room. It gave us a few precious moments alone. Besides, the guards loved to visit with the children.

Both of us tried hard to make the children feel as secure as possible under the circumstances.

We deliberately kept from them the everyday details. They were sure that daddy would be home soon and that some Turkish person somehow just got things mixed up.

Why Us, God?

It was difficult to fight the feeling of, "*Why us, God? Why have you abandoned us?*"

Somedays, I even began to question if there really was a God. Deep down inside I knew the answer...but.

God may have chosen us because he knew our family was strong enough to maybe make it through this ordeal. Perhaps someone else might not. I was in no way happy about his choice, mind you, but I guessed there was a reason.

I knew all this in my mind and heart but the rest of me was 'still a little ticked off at God' right then.

Like a little kid...I wanted it now, now, now. I wanted my husband home. I wanted us all to be back together and to have a normal life. I was tired, tired, tired of this.

The little girl within me was scared. The woman was determined. The mother was anguished for my children and frustrated that I could not protect them from having to go through this ordeal. The wife within me was terrified for her spouse.

"Perhaps in the years to come, I might appreciate what this lesson in Turkey is teaching me. Perhaps someday I would be thankful for my course in Middle East Survival 101. But, right now, folks, I would not place a bet."

So, I told myself, "*Okay Winston, I'll stop feeling sorry for myself and my family. I'll put my sneakers back on; keep on walking softly and carrying our two new big sticks. I will try to keep a stiff upper lip and get on with it—whatever 'it' may bring tomorrow.*"

"Tonight I am being selfish. Tonight I am eating the last Ho Ho! Sorry, kids!"

I went to bed, wrapped myself in Chase's terrycloth housecoat and soon, had a full night's sleep for the first time in a while.

Tourists

Before I drifted off to sleep that night, my mind went to the tourists in Istanbul who were soaking in the quaint, exotic, mysterious experience at the Istanbul Hilton. They were unaware of the drama unfolding for other Americans only a few hundred miles away. They were oblivious of the danger that perhaps they, too, could be arrested on some trumped up charge and become the next hostage.

I prayed that they all stayed safe. Yet, I longed to be in their shoes because they had plane tickets and a departure date!

I wondered what, my love, was thinking...if he was awake?

These thoughts would need to wait until tomorrow for it was time for me to fall asleep.

I almost forgot, *"Oh, yes, thank you, God, for those two big sticks today!"*

Reflections

The next morning I woke up just before dawn and my mind drifted back to *that morning*.

I could not believe that in a few weeks our whole world changed so completely.

Only a few nights before this hell began, Chase and I were having our evening glass of iced tea on the porch, watching the traffic on the ancient cobblestone road out front. The road out front once was part of the Appian Way. To think there had been so many invading forces that had passed on that very road.

Still, in this modern day, we could sit on our porch and see this impressive sight: The rugged looking Kurdish men dressed in their leather vests astride their tall stallions with their guns slung across their backs as they rode in front of our house. Their guns were covered and wrapped in fur pelts but it was obvious what they were.

The Turkish authorities never seemed to bother the Kurds as they drifted from country to country. Nor, did they bother the Gypsy tribes as they wandered back and forth across the borders, it would seem.

As we sat there, we could almost hear the same clomp of horses' hooves and see the Roman soldiers riding down this same road so many, many years ago.

Each morning, the street bustled with horse-drawn carts filled high with baskets and chickens and all sorts of wares. We watched the occasional car or truck dart in and out between them.

It was strange to see the contrast between this ancient and modern world—both co-existing yet each vying for their own small place in this society.

I understood that with the exception of a few telephones, a few cars and trucks, and electricity in the cities times had not changed much over the years. Istanbul, of course, did not represent what Turkish culture was for the rest of the country. Istanbul was much more, Europeanized.

Since Ataturk, there were changes in some of the laws and ways of life. This was a culture, which outwardly seemed changed but fundamentally remained the same.

We must remember this was Turkey's culture. This was their belief system. This was their religion and their country. Did we really have the right to judge them by our own belief systems?

Likewise, Cyprus had her own culture that was quite different from the culture, belief system, and religion of the Turks. We, unfortunately, were caught up in their strife. We were wedged in the triangle within the politics of not only these two countries but of our own America.

Of one thing I am quite certain—the more I traveled the world and learned about other countries, the more I saw their differences. However, the more I realized they were all much the same in one way. Each was convinced that their culture and their religion was the one and only right one.

I saw in this world that most people believe in a higher power—be it Christian, Jewish, Muslim, or Buddhist. I have met wonderful loving, caring people and found positive, as well as negative, in all these cultures.

I wondered, *"If a belief is different from ours, should it automatically be condemned as wrong?"*

As long as a belief is not doing harm to their followers or people of other religions or other countries who are we to judge? It only means it is different by our standards and beliefs.

I cannot condemn the Turks for their culture. As an American, it certainly was not my choice. It was unnerving, to say the least, to be placed in the position we were in—subjects of this foreign culture that was so alien to us.

Enough philosophy, I went back to sleep.

A Little Bit of Peace

Finally, I awoke feeling as if I could catch my breath for the first time in weeks. It was a quiet Saturday morning and, for the moment, there was a sense of peace.

The children came and snuggled in my bed, as they were used to doing most weekend mornings when we were home in the States. Sometimes they would spend an hour or so, just talking about whatever they had on their minds or kidding with each other until Chase and I threw them out. Those were wonderful times.

"If only Chase were here. I know he must miss this so!"

The Ol' College Try

Come Monday morning, I got another summons to appear in *His office.*

I was more than tired of surprises. It was getting old having that panicked feeling in the pit of my stomach when *He* summoned me. I could only guess that *He* was ticked off about the two big sticks on Friday. I figured I would probably be chastised for going over the authority's head. But, ask me if I cared?

Secretly, I could hardly wait to see his face. I should not, could not, and would not snicker—at least not aloud.

By this time, I was quite familiar with the S.O.P. when I went into the room. The two other men exchanged niceties for about one minute and then they were, dismissed.

Then, *He* started that "Honey" thing again.

"Honey, I admire all that you have been doing. You have already done more than your husband could expect of any wife in supporting him."

"Honey, you will be happy to know 'I' have made special arrangements for your husband's pay and allowances to be continued. I will see to it that the children and you can stay on base until you choose to leave."

He never mentioned the telegrams. *He* did not know I knew about them, let alone that I had a copy of the originals in my purse at that very moment!

This man was rather like a puppy that had just pooped on the carpet in front of everybody.

Oh, how I would have liked to have rubbed his nose in it. I will admit, *He* gave it 'the ol' college try' in hoping to convince me to go home, yet again. He told me of the grave mistake that I was making for my husband's sake, if we stayed.

He was so concerned for us! *Sweet dear!*

I played his little game. I diplomatically thanked him for his time and concern on my way out the door.

In no manner was I flip or rude to *Him* because I knew that that would not be wise at all. *They* and *He* and their power over our lives could not be discounted.

Although we now had the support and help of Washington and the Pentagon—those were only two of many voices. Furthermore, those voices might not be heard all the way across that big pond.

Those two voices were *there* and we were *here*.

Each Had to Cope

The business of daily living went on. We still had a long way to go until the next hearing date for Chase. The days seem to drag on to infinity; they moved agonizingly slowly for both of us. We each had to cope with our own set of problems.

The prison was almost starting to feel like our second home. The children and I still went every day. Each time we left, I felt Chase growing just a little bit more distant. It was as though, deep inside, he was jealous that we were free to go…*"If the truth be known, most of us would probably feel the same."*

I was thankful that Chase was in the political prison

section. It was a more civilized atmosphere—if you could call a Turkish prison civilized.

From what I have read, a Turkish prison was much different from our American prisons. The sanitary conditions were woefully lacking and there was no heat or air-conditioning as well as no hot water. In the heat of the day, when the temperature was 100 plus degrees, the prisoners would wait for the soothing coolness of early morning (about 2:00 a.m.) before they could fall asleep.

One of the challenging aspects of everyday life for Chase and his roommates was lack of things to keep them occupied. He exercised a lot and they were allowed to play cards and read.

It was difficult for men who were used to being productive to be so idle.

Most all his roommates had unbelievably interesting stories to tell. I enjoyed the tales of some of their escapades. Some were rather funny and some quite tragic.

It was interesting what a sense of humor some had about their imprisonment. A couple of men had been caught running contraband several times. Their attitude seemed to be that getting caught and imprisoned was the hazard of their profession.

Preparation

The children were scheduled to start school next month. The next hearing date was scheduled for the day after school would commence.

The children and I went about accomplishing the normal school preparation. We bought a few clothes—or at least as many as the Base Exchange had in stock and our budget would allow. The supplies in the BX were very limited. Since I liked to sew, I would make what we could not buy—if I could find the material.

Besides, sewing kept me occupied at night when the children were in bed. I found it hard to fall asleep until the early morning so I thought I might as well be productive.

Chase said that he woke up most nights still hearing the gunshots from *that morning*. I did as well sometimes. Worse, yet, he still relived the beatings he took at the hands of the local police and he now had to live with some hearing loss in one ear as a result.

There were so many possible scenarios to consider when and if Chase was safely back with us. Would we leave Turkey right away? Would they make us stay? If we did go back home, I wondered where our next assignment would be? Would they let him stay in the military? If not, what will we do? At least with him being in the medical field, he would always have a job.

The Unofficial, Official Word

The telephone rang. I turned off the radio and answered it but there was no voice on the other end. I figured someone had misdialed.

I had gotten used to having the radio turned on. I put the radio close to the 'bug' in our trailer so no one could hear every word we said.

Realistically, I think they were only interested in my telephone conversations, if any. I often wondered if a neighbor might have been recruited to let *them* know when I had a visitor.

A few minutes later Imp and I went out in the yard to play ball. Mack drove up and said we needed to talk where we did not have any ears. I got Imp a water bottle, a snack and her stroller. Off we went to the flight line. I drove our car and Mack drove his.

As we walked along the road adjacent to the flight line, Mack told me that it was still important for us to carry on our conversations in a secure area. Mack had heard our quarters were still bugged.

In the middle of our conversation, my mind wandered. It dawned on me that for every action there was a reaction. I was formulating a plan to, perhaps, mitigate the problem or at least bring a little levity into my life .

They would get my reaction to my telephone being bugged. I would call my neighbor and describe to her in vivid detail the color and odor of the baby's poop and throw-up. Then perhaps I would ask her if it was a normal color, etcetera. I would say anything that I could think of that would turn someone off from wanting to listen to my conversations.

I do not know if it had any effect but it made my day thinking of them turning green while listening to the details.

I had to ask Mack to forgive me. My attention had drifted while he was talking. I was a little embarrassed that I needed to ask him to repeat what he had just said.

Mack had been trying to explain to me that a big meeting with the U.S. and high-up Turkish officials was scheduled for the week before, Chase's hearing.

The dates were not a coincidence. The other two men's hearings would also be on the same day. It was unofficially, official that these men were to be used for leverage... *"As if we did not already know of the Turk's intent."*

Mack said that no one he had spoken to knew for sure what the American official position would be.

Although I could have called Ed Gurney from the base, I thought it best that I call from our Turkish friend's house.

That evening I left a note in the clothesline. I asked our friend to meet me tomorrow in the little village nearby at about two o'clock.

The note back from our friend said, "Tomorrow, yes. We are looking to see you in the afternoon."

I would have to forgo seeing Chase. Instead of using the normal driver, I called Mack and asked him to drive me to see Chase. Obviously, I could not tell him over the phone that I had another plan to meet our friend and use the phone. I told Mack I needed to meet earlier than usual.

Mack told his office staff that he had legal matters to talk over with Chase. When Mack picked me up he said, "What the heck are you up to now?" I explained. He agreed and so he dropped me off in the village. He continued on to see Chase to explain why I had not come to visit.

Mack and I planned to meet in four hours where he dropped me off.

Escalation

Our friend's gardener picked me up at the village and drove me quickly to their house to use their phone. Because of the time difference between the East Coast of the U.S. and Turkey, I had no time to waste.

When I tried to call Ed's office the phone rang and rang. Finally, Ed's Secretary answered. As soon as I told her who I was, she put me through immediately to him.

"Hello, Sondra," Ed said, "Good to hear from you

personally. How is Chase? How can I help?"

Before I had time to say a word, he said he had intel for me about the cause of the escalation of the Anti-American problem over Cyprus. The escalation had precipitated the American military men's arrest.

The U.S. learned of Turkey's plans to invade Cyprus on June 5th or 6th of 1964. President Johnson sent a letter to the Turkish government stating, in his now infamous letter of June 5, 1964, that he would not come to the aid of Turkey if the invasion of Cyprus led to conflict with Russia. The letter had been a knee-jerk reaction from Johnson according to the history books.

George Ball of the Diplomatic Corporation described the letter as being the diplomatic equivalent of an atom bomb. Sterns called it a specimen of diplomatic overkill.

Now we knew why Chase's arrest had come about within a few days after Johnson's letter. The Turkish Government was totally ticked off.

When I finally got a chance to speak, I told Ed of the latest developments with Chase and the fact that the officials continued to want to make the children and me go home.

Ed said he would call General Lemay's office as soon as I hung up, "To put a stop to some of this idiocy," or as much as he had the power to control.

Tea and Trouble

I hung up and went into the living room where our friends were sitting. They asked me to stay a little while to share tea with them and talk.

It was good to see our Turkish friends. It was comforting to sit there in their huge house, drinking hot, red Turkish tea out of a glass cup and eating Baklava, as we so often did.

Oh, how I enjoyed the sweet smell of homemade rose water towels used to wipe off our hands afterward.

His wife, the dear sweet woman, gave me an Eye of Allah necklace to protect us.

She leaned over and touched my hand in an attempt to send comfort to all of us in our family. They were both, in their own way, trying to apologize for what had happened to us in their country.

They told me bluntly that the word from Ankara, the capital, was Chase was not to be freed of the charges and that those charges probably would get worse.

He told me certain people were working on a plan to get the Turkish judge to release Chase to the base until the final court date. He then informed me the Turkish lawyer was their personal friend. To this, I said a "*Thanks, God*" to myself.

The Turkish lawyer had told them that if Chase were to be released he would not be allowed to leave the country. He spoke also of the coming negotiations. He warned me again that Turkish ways were very slow.

I shivered, as a cold chill took over me from the last words he had spoken concerning not leaving the country.

He cautioned me again about allowing anyone to know of our friendship or that we were still in contact.

They sent me back to the base with a big basket of vegetables, fruit, and the children's favorite Turkish food—a special flatbread that had just come right out of the oven. Their gardener drove me downtown to the bazaar and put me into a taxi that was waiting to take me back to meet Mack.

The children were pleased with the goodies. It helped

to make up for the fact I had not let them go see their dad. I did not tell the children where the treats had come from just in case they should ever let it slip.

Do I Tell Him or Not?

That night, I had a hard decision to make. Was I going to tell Chase about the conversation I had had with our friend? I decided not to because Chase needed to have hope.

I did tell him about the conversation with Ed—at least the part about him getting in contact with General Lemay to help in "This lunacy."

At least, if he could be released to the base, that would be a gigantic step. It appeared our friend was reasonably sure that this could be accomplished.

Their family had influence although I did not fully realize how powerful and how much they were willing to risk for us. At this point, I was becoming quite cynical at my 'now old age' of twenty-six.

Not knowing whom I could trust, I decided it would be better not to let the right hand know what the left hand was doing. Nor was it prudent to tell our Turkish friends about Ed Gurney or General Lemay.

That night, all I could think about was if Chase would be released to the base. Would that be a signal that this would soon be resolved?

The Straw that Could Break the Camel's Back

Mother sent a letter to me. I had not written to Mother about what had happened. I had only told her we had moved on base. She had no idea of our ordeal.

Mother's letter said that she had taken a ship to

Europe and bought a new car, an Opel, in Germany. She was going to drive down to Turkey to see us. She did not know exactly when she would arrive but it would be in a few weeks.

Then, I got the lecture about how I had not written enough and how I seemed to have completely forgotten her.

It was true. I had not written to her since *that morning,* except to say we had moved on base, I did not know what to say, nor did I want to lie to her.

When I looked at the date on the envelope, I almost panicked. It had been written two weeks ago! She could be here any day. I had no way to stop her travel plans.

All we needed now was Mother and her attitude. She would be most put out that we would not be able to do tourist things in order to entertain her. Understandably, she would also be unhappy because I had not told her about our ordeal.

The worst part was that she could be dangerous to our cause. Mother could and probably would stir up the pot on both sides if she decided to get involved.

Mother did not have the foggiest idea about military life and she sure as heck would not accept her role as a woman in Turkey. Worse yet, she was a woman driving alone. Mother was not a person who knew what the word 'no' meant.

What's more, Chase was not home to be a buffer. When he was around, she rarely pulled her little tricks. Normally, I could handle Mother but not right now.

This new wrinkle in our lives could have been the straw that broke this camel's back.

I wondered, tongue in cheek, if Chase had an empty bed in his dorm. I could become jealous of his secure position right now!

Our mother-daughter thing notwithstanding, I wondered how would I possibly help her now if she encountered some kind of a problem. I could only hope that she stayed safe.

The one positive aspect was the car she had just purchased in Germany had German license plates. The Turks did not mess with the Germans.

The reason the Turks did not mess with the Germans was that there were many Turks living and working in Germany. I understood that the German way of assuring their citizens were treated with respect was the mathematical formula 'one equals three.' A Turk messing with one German equated to Germany messing with three Turks who lived in Germany.

"Where do I sign us up to be German?"

In order for Mother to get onto the base when she arrived, I would have to leave a message at the gate.

I was hoping for a miracle, some viable excuse, but I found none. It felt as if it were a plot against us. So having found no way out, I drove down to the front gate and left a message to allow Mother through. I left her directions to our quarters.

My only hope was that Mother might possibly show her compassionate side if and when she heard what was happening to her family.

"Right now, I could certainly use an ally."

Turns out, Mother was a no-show for a while.

Now, on top of our worrying about the next court date, we had deep concerns for Mother's safety. We had no way of contacting her to find out where she was or if she was ok.

"Please let this adventurous Mother of mine be safe!"

Chapter 12
Court Date 2

It was good that we were busy the last few days before the next court date.

Mia and CJ were looking forward to getting back to school. They were into the normal stage of "I'm bored and nothing to do attitude" that most children have by the end of summer.

They were, needless to say, concerned about whether we would be going right back to the States and where we might be stationed for our next tour.

I felt very frustrated at not being able to give them a definite answer about our move and their school. I wanted to know as well.

The last few days before the trial, Mack came by when he could on his break. We had coffee and we talked about superficial things. He did not have much real news but his friendship helped.

School and Rumors

The children started school. They were a bit put off when several of their classmates started questioning them about the incident with their dad.

CJ and Mia had been rather sheltered from peer

pressures of this type so far. Their out-of-school contact with other children had been limited to a couple of their immediate friends who knew all about it and knew their dad was a good guy.

One of CJ's classmates made some comments about Chase being a "Jailbird" which really made CJ mad and protective of his Dad! CJ was crushed that someone would think his Dad had done something wrong.

I went to the teacher the next day before school and explained what had happened. I asked her to allow me to talk with the class. She kindly gave me permission and asked if there was anything else, she could do to help?

After my visit to class, we never had any further problems with any of the children. CJ's classmates became supportive and understanding.

The classmates would always want to get the latest update, which CJ really did not particularly want to share. We came up with a statement for our children to issue that would satisfy their classmates' and, I suspected, their parents' curiosity.

Catch Twenty-Two

I was trapped in a catch twenty-two situation. If I shared my fears with anyone then I was branded a hysterical woman, incapable of handling the difficulties at hand.

However, if I put on a good front for the world to see, it seemed to turn people off from being sympathetic to our cause. It looked to them like I evidently had no problems.

Sam's wife told me that a woman saw me in the BX one day and said that I was smiling and spending lots of money. She felt my attitude, under the circumstances, was appalling. She also told my friend that she believed that I thought that I was better than everyone else was and that I did not want anybody's help.

She did not happen to mention that the money I was spending was for school clothes. By the way, she was one of the women that had wanted to farm out the children that first night on base.

I can understand her reaction based upon my rejection of their offer to take the children and split us up that night. In all fairness, I believe the women that night had good intentions.

I longed to be with people who really knew me. I needed a friend to hug me. I needed to be able to hug back. I especially missed my friend Sara Nell back in Florida. We had been best friends for years. There was never anything that we could not or did not share. Our lives had always run uncannily parallel. When I had a baby, so did she. If her children got the chickenpox so did mine. When Chase was promoted so was her husband even though he was not in the military and had no connection career-wise.

"What is happening to my dear sweet Sara Nell right now? Are she and her family going through hell, as we are now?"

The Night Before C D 2

The night before Court Day Two, I could not sleep. My saner side said not to set myself up for disappointment but my heart was full of excitement and hope.

Nonetheless, I did fix a special dinner so that all I would have to do is warm it up the next day. I knew that either way I would not want to have to cook. Besides, it kept me busy.

Cleaning house and fussing with all the details kept

me occupied until 2:00 a.m. when I sunk into bed exhausted. Although sleep was not to be for me all night, I did manage to get a bit of rest and quiet time.

I could not wait until the time to get up and start the day—the day for which I had so yearned. The day when Chase might finally be released and we could have our lives back, once again, at least for a little while.

At long last, the light peeked through and around the edges of the bedroom blinds. It was time to start this day I had so long awaited.

C D 2 Begins

The children went to school with the promise from me that I would come to school right after court to let them know the outcome.

They wanted to go with me but it was certainly no place for them to be.

Mack picked me up and we drove to the courthouse. He gave me little hope for the day's outcome. He was, in his own way, preparing me for Chase not being released or worse.

Mack's words kept ringing in my ears, *"What did he mean by worse?"*

This time in court we were even more apprehensive and worried about Chase's safety! Based on how he had been manhandled before, we did not know what to expect!

Then, there was that "or worse" comment from Mack.

I wondered, *"Had our Turkish friends been wrong? Was there really no hope of Chase being released to the base, at least? Had Mack been told something he was not sharing with me?"*

We entered the large old courtroom. It was filled with

Turkish people—mostly men.

The atmosphere was very dissimilar to the previous time. There was a low hissing sound coming from some of the Turkish people sitting in the seats as we walked down the aisle.

We could hardly find an empty seat because there were so many people. We walked all the way to the front row and turned around to head to the back. It appeared that we would have to stand at the back of the room.

As we headed to the back, two men moved over to let us in the second row. Soon everyone else in the row exited after we sat down. Within a few minutes, the people that had moved over to let us sit left as well. It was as if we had the plague.

Looking down at the seat, I realized we had been sitting in this same spot before. The bloodstain from my hand was still on the wooden bench.

In the front row was Chase's new Turkish lawyer who had actually never consulted with Chase before today. It was not the same man. This man was not our Turkish friend's lawyer—our ally!

How could this lawyer even begin to protect or support Chase? Did he have even the slightest clue of what has gone on with this case?

Mack and I both were disappointed to see only one other American present and neither of us recognized the man. The officer came over, sat next to Mack, introduced himself and after that did not say another word. Mack looked at me as if to say, "What the heck is this guy all about?" We were surprised and annoyed that he was wearing an Air Force uniform and not civilian clothes…We were both thinking, "*Was he stupid?*"

It did not appear that other Americans were present

or at least that we could recognize.

We sat there for over an hour. It was hot and the odors from all the bodies packed in a room with no open windows were nauseating. Both Mack and I were trying not to throw up... Their deodorant had definitely run out.

I leaned over with my nose pushed against one hand trying to stop the smell from going in at least one nostril while breathing through my mouth. I was trying not to be too obvious and offend anyone.

As we sat there, we were soon distracted by cockroaches that were running back and forth across the aisle... They were the entertainment for the crowd until the real circus would begin.

Finally, the tall, heavy door flew open and in came ten heavily armed guards with rifles in hand. That hissing sound came again from the Turkish people, but now much louder, as Chase was brought forward!

It appeared the guards were from the Turkish Army. Their uniforms were different from the ones worn by the guards at the previous court date.

Their attitude was different—they had a definite military bearing about them.

Two more guards escorted Chase down the long middle aisle. Chase was both handcuffed and shackled.

I wanted to scream at them. I hated them with all my being for what they were doing to my Chase!

Chase knew not to try to look around.

He was brought in front of the judge who had just entered the room and climbed up on his little perch.

The Turkish lawyer was summoned to speak with the judge for a few minutes. It was quite apparent that the Turkish lawyer was very upset as he listened to the judge!

They were in a serious conversation. It was mostly the judge grumbling at the lawyer about something.

The judge motioned to the guards with a flip of his hand as if to say, "Get this man away from me!"

The guards grabbed Chase forcefully and put him into a seat in front of the judge!

The lawyer went back to his seat in front and as he did, he looked at Mack and shook his head very slightly back and forth.

Something was very wrong. It was apparent from the lawyer's body language.

Then, a Turkish man was brought into the room assisted by another man. He had a large bandage on his left arm and it was in a sling. He appeared to be in great pain.

This *man* seemed familiar, but *from where?*

Mack and I both guessed that they were evidently hearing other cases before Chase's. We could only wonder if that was the reason that the courtroom was so crowded.

To us, it seemed to be a good sign. Perhaps Chase was no longer was the star attraction.

Did we dare hope this might be over in a few minutes or hours?

We assumed that the Turkish lawyer was shaking his head because Chase's case was not the next to be heard and not because he had just received bad news. What a relief!

As to the poor man standing before the judge, I assumed they had decided to hear his case first. I wondered if he was the defendant or the plaintiff. We did not see anyone else around who appeared to be with this man other than his friend who was helping to support him.

The judge spoke with the man for two or three minutes.

Mack and I were not fluent enough in the Turkish language to understand what was being spoken. Besides, the judge was too far away to hear even if we did speak fluent Turkish.

Some of the Turkish people in the other side of the front row, closer to the judge, gasped with obvious sympathy for this man!

Mack and I did hear the word American uttered several times in his short conversation with the judge. The word American came across loud and clear.

We both wondered why the man was here and what had happened to him. Whatever it was, it must have been severe and it obviously involved an American. There did not seem to be any other Americans in the room—at least that we could see from where we were sitting.

Suddenly, the judge motioned for Chase and the Turkish lawyer to stand up. I assumed it was time for Chase's case to come before the court. The case with the other man did not seem to take long.

The guards moved toward Chase. For a second, I thought they were going to do something violent to him. I felt Mack instinctively starting to get up from his seat to help Chase, but he knew he could not. Mack reluctantly sat back down and clenched his fists.

Next, two guards grabbed Chase's arms and jerked him up out of his seat and placed him in front of the judge. The judge called for the Turkish lawyer to come forward. The judge then proceeded to speak quite sternly to the lawyer for almost five minutes.

This time Mack and I could hear but we still could not understand. I picked up the words, prison, children, and

Incirlik toward the end (Incirlik was the name of the base, as well as the little town just outside the main gate).

The judge told the Turkish lawyer to translate for Chase. He asked Chase if he owned a gun. Chase answered, "Yes." He asked Chase if he had shot the man that had been in the courtroom before. Chase said, "Of course not and that we..." But before Chase could get the rest of the story out of his mouth, "We were the ones who had been shot at," the judge yelled at Chase to "Dur" (stop, be silent).

The judge spoke with great authority about something for no more than a minute to the audience. In general, he seemed to be addressing Chase and his lawyer. The judge then flicked his hand, telling the guards to take Chase out!

The Turkish crowd was obviously pleased with what the judge had said!

The guards allowed the Turkish lawyer barely one minute to say something to Chase. Chase's face went white as they escorted him past us toward the door!

His eyes met mine as he left the courtroom. I could not tell what he was trying to say to me!

"Oh, God! Where on earth are they taking him? Why is he not being released?"

What Now? What Next!

The Turkish lawyer took Mack and me to a small, dingy room to get away from the crowd. The people were not particularly threatening right then but we needed privacy for a few minutes. Also the old saying, "Out of sight, out of mind," was the best avenue to pursue right this minute.

The lawyer said the judge was, in fact, releasing Chase to the custody of the base officials. The judge said that he could see that Chase was a good husband and family man.

He, the judge, understood that his wife and children had come to visit him each day in prison and, therefore, he was a good father. He also felt it was too hard on his children to continue this for now.

I prayed, *"Thank you, God!"* Our daily visits to the prison had seemingly attained the impression we had wanted. Our tireless procession each day paid off in two ways—in our support of Chase, we had made a good impression.

The lawyer then told us of the judge's other decision. Chase had been charged with "Attempted murder" of that man in court! If convicted by the Turkish court, Chase could spend the rest of his life in a Turkish prison, at best. At worst, he could be put to death by a firing squad!

What, then, was all that rhetoric about? "Chase being a good father" and "How his poor family had been through enough!" Was it just some vain attempt to make the Turkish court look as though it had some humanity? At least until they killed the poor children's father!

The substance of what the lawyer had just told us was mindboggling. I could hardly think or feel or breathe!

Both Mack and I sat down and were silent for a while. There were no words.

The next trial date was set for six months later.

We were so overwhelmed by this new twist; I actually forgot that Chase was being released!

Chase's Turkish lawyer brought me back from my stupefied state when he said that we could meet Chase at the prison in about an hour at which time he should be released.

The lawyer suggested that we not waste a moment. He gently shook my shoulder and asked if I wanted some water. He said that I looked as white as a sheet. I excused myself, stumbled to the restroom and splashed cold water on my face while trying not to throw up or faint!

A few minutes later (when I was back in the room with Mack) he said we needed to get Chase out of the prison before somebody changed their mind. I concurred with what he said.

The negotiations with Cyprus and the U.S. were obviously moving slowly and not to Turkish liking, it would seem. They were trying to buy time. The Turkish government still needed their American hostages for leverage.

I knew then that we had our Turkish friend to thank for Chase's release from prison and transfer to the confines of the base.

All the mixed messages from the judge had our minds reeling. First release Chase to the base and then bring him up on attempted murder charges at the next trial date, all in the same breath!

The Turkish lawyer said he was going out to talk to the prison officials to make arrangements. He said he recommended that we get another car or two to accompany us to the prison as escorts, just in case.

We did not know why the Turkish lawyer wanted us to have escorts at the prison. Americans would have no authority to protect Chase or anyone else. If anything, they would be in danger as well. We decided he must have his reasons.

Mack and I followed the lawyer's request. We went to the base and requisitioned two more civilian looking cars with four Air Policemen in each car. They were, of course, not in uniform. Then hurriedly, we all drove down to the prison.

There was not enough time to tell the children that their dad would be home shortly after school was finished for the day. How happy would those little people be? At long last, Daddy would be home!

As Mack and I pulled up to the prison there was already another official Air Force car in front. Mack was allowed to go help Chase clear out his dorm room of his few possessions. Chase left most of his things, what little he had, for the others to share.

His fellow prisoners hugged and kissed Chase goodbye. They asked if they could all take turns coming to the window, as they usually did when the children and I visited, to say goodbye.

We stayed a few minutes longer so I could wave goodbye to each of them as they took their turn at the barred window in the door.

Reality vs Fantasy

I had imagined this moment when Chase would be released. I had replayed this scene again and again in my mind for months.

Chase would hug and kiss me passionately and we would walk hand in hand out the prison gate, relieved that this was all over—that we would be going home soon.

We would then go back to base and be alone for the first time in months before we got the children out of school.

In reality, it went like this: We were facing a life in prison or death sentence—plus another six months under the thumb of the Turkish Government! At least Chase would be physically on the base with us!

Our reunion was not quite "our reunion!" At best, it

was just a short reprieve. I reminded myself, "*Whichever it is, we will take it for the moment.*"

Chase was still as numb as I was. We were quite relieved that he had been released from prison, but we were completely overwhelmed by the new charges.

He gave me a somewhat pre-occupied hug and kiss when I came into the prison. After that, the base officials took over.

I thought that Chase's response was understandable, I guess. But secretly, there was part of me that felt very disappointed. I had fought so hard and was willing to risk so much! I was feeling very left out. Right that moment, I needed assurance of Chase's love for me.

We were driven back to the base in separate cars. Chase was taken to *The Office* for debriefing.

Our neighbor saw them drop me off and brought Imp home to me. I told her, "Daddy would be home in a little while." She squeezed with delight.

Imp and I immediately went to pick up Mia and CJ after school. They were beyond happy at the prospect of finally having Daddy home. I hoped the debriefing would not take too long and he would be home before they burst with excitement!

I did not tell anyone about the new charges at this point. I simply was not up to uttering the words, "Life in prison or firing squad."

I had hoped Chase and I would have at least an hour or so alone, to hold each other and to talk before we had to take on the parent role—before we had to start acting as if everything was okay. I knew we were going to have to continue to take life as we had for the last few months—one day and one hurdle at a time.

For today, however, we would just be grateful that we

would all be back together and breathe in this feeling of relief, albeit tenuous.

Tomorrow—we could think about tomorrow.

Chapter 13
At Long Last

The children got busy making Welcome Home signs for Dad before he arrived.

It had seemed like an infinity of time had passed since *that morning*. And likewise too long since this morning, when Chase had driven in the other car away from the prison.

Finally a car pulled up into the drive. The door opened and there stood our Chase—back home with us again. The children fought each other to get out of the door— each wanting to be the first to hug their dad.

We ate the special dinner that I had cooked the night before with all of Chase's favorite foods. For the first time in ages, all his food was actually hot. The children asked their dad, if they could have Ho Hos for dessert and make their special coffee, too?

Chase managed his usual wink at Mom as the children sipped their coffee. I almost burst out crying at that sight.

The children were so excited that it took what seemed like forever, before we could get them all settled down for the night.

We were emotionally wrung out and thankful when our little crew finally fell asleep.

Chase had the luxury for the first time in a long time of having a hot shower and a comfortable bed. It was wonderful to be together and away from the rest of the world.

Wonderful to be Just Us

Somehow "*us*" had changed. Chase seemed to be distracted and somewhat distant. It seemed almost as though he felt he did not belong or maybe he just needed to be alone for a while.

It had been a very long day. We were spent, both mentally and physically, and discussion of what had happened or what would happen in our future would have to wait until tomorrow.

Exhausted, Chase was fast asleep in bed before I finished my shower. I snuggled around his back to reassure myself that he was truly there beside me once again.

The following morning before the children woke up we spoke quietly in our bedroom so as not to let the children overhear our conversation.

Chase told me about his debriefing the day before. He was warned that there was no chance that he or we would be whisked away back to the U.S.

They would have to hold him here on the base. There would be no 'flying us all out in the dark of the night.' They warned that if we tried to escape back to the States, by Turkish-American law, a.k.a., Status of Forces Agreement, they would return Chase back to Turkey.

It was going to take time for Chase to adjust to this way of life again. It was understandable as this was an enormous contrast to the nightmare he had been living in since *that morning*.

The everyday problems of life seemed so superficial and unimportant when a person is living in a crisis.

It became vividly clear that it would be difficult to get back to being a normal family again. I recall thinking, "*At this point, I do not know if we even remember what normal looks like.*"

Although we had become good at putting on a happy face for the world to see, it was much more difficult to put on a happy face inside our quarters—especially when we were alone. The adjustment process was even worse when we knew that at any moment, it could all be taken away.

I wondered what was happening to our 'oneness.' Was it slipping away?

On the next morning, there was another note in the clothesline. It read, "Our happiness is for your together being. We are most relieved."

I sent them back a thank you note expressing our love and wishing them well.

Chapter 14
Together for Christmas

The In-Between of C D 2 and C D 3

Mother showed up at the base a week after Chase was released. I was relieved that Chase was home and I did not have to handle her by myself. Mother was normally on her best behavior around Chase.

Lucky for me Chase's commander had given him ten days off to adjust and recover.

Mother was not about to admit that she should not be driving by herself. I had warned her about the attitude toward women in Turkey in my letter to her some time back.

We tried to impress on Mother how concerned we had been about her driving in Turkey. She in turn denied that she had had any trouble as a woman driving in Turkey...We knew better.

Later our suspicions were confirmed as she finally admitted she had several narrow escapes on the way from Istanbul to Adana. We could only assume the German plates on the Opel she had just purchased in Munich had saved her little posterior.

We had not told her what was really going on with us— what hell we had and were going through. As we really were not doing much socializing, it was easy to keep our secret as long as she did not come in contact with anyone who could, spill the beans.

Chase told her that many of the base personnel with high-security clearances were restricted to the base. Not knowing anything about the military, she did not know the difference. Chase told her the restriction to base included their families for security reasons.

Mother stayed for about a week and then went on her way. She left in somewhat of a huff because we had chosen not to take her to see the sights around Adana.

We felt guilty being untruthful to her especially since she had come so far to visit...but we were cowards...I know.

Mother would probably have insisted on staying until the trial out of curiosity, if nothing else. She would have been miserable being confined to the base with us. There was also the added problem of having no room for her to stay long-term in our already cramped quarters.

Bless Mother, but at that particular moment, we could not have handled any additional drama!

And Life Went On

Chase went back to duty a few days after Mother left.

Given that the hospital was only a couple of blocks from our quarters, Chase came home each day for lunch, which gave us time to talk without our children to overhear. I tried to put Imp down for her nap early if I could.

There were some days when our lives almost seemed at peace.

In reality, we were hard-pressed to define "peace" at this point. For us, it meant emotionally surviving the day—especially with C D 3 hanging over our heads!

Fortunately, there was school for the children, work for Chase, and the normal Mom things for me to fill our days.

There were, however, a few diversions.

Upon several occasions a local Turkish man was allowed to bring his camel to school for the children to see or ride, if they so choose. Most of the classmates opted only to look at the camel from afar.

One particular camel had a nasty personality and spit a lot if anyone dared to get close. As any of you camel owners know—camels do have a habit of spitting that is most unpleasant.

Luckily, on another occasion, the camel owner brought a different camel with a much more pleasant temperament. She seemed to actually like, the children's attention.

Mia and CJ both mustered up their "American can-do Spirit," climbed up, and took a spin. This camel had one hump, which did not make as comfy a ride as a two-hump camel, I was told. Since they were not crossing the Sahara desert on a long trek, I figured it really was of no consequence and that their tushes would survive.

These two new explorers could now add "camel riders" to their repertoire of experiences in Turkey.

Oh, how pleased they were with themselves. You would have thought that they were pioneers in a new world.

The camel became emotionally attached to Mia and CJ and even tried to follow them when they started to leave the playground.

As a result, the children then pleaded to have her for their pet. They assured us that they would tie her up on the clothesline and 'they' would feed her.

Their pleading was to no avail since any parent knows that old line "I will feed my pet if only you will let me have it."

Mia and CJ were most annoyed and claimed that they had cruel parents who would not allow them to have a camel for a pet, at least until they returned to the States, "you could hear the violins playing".

Our entertainment most evenings was watching a couple of hours of TV. The base did have a TV station of sorts. It was canned TV and nothing except the announcer was live. Canned TV meant that the films of the programs were sent over to the base in cans, which was not exactly a highly technical process.

Even these few hours a day with a couple of programs helped to keep us updated and gave us a small sense of being back home.

There was a movie theater called the Oasis. Most of the times there was only one movie shown a week. Occasionally, they would have a special kid's movie on Saturday morning.

After a few months, we all were suffering from a major case of Cabin Fever or in this case Base Fever—so any diversion helped.

In essence, Chase was still a prisoner and subsequently so were we. Chase could not leave the base. Legally he could with permission from the Turks, but it would not have been a prudent thing to do at all.

Work-wise Chase's situation was as normal as possible under the circumstances. Everyone in his squadron had a very 'business as usual' and friendly attitude toward Chase.

Socially, we were still hot potatoes. Most people were

still afraid to be associated with us. I did occasionally have a few women at the children's school tell me personally about how "they sympathized with us" and "wished they could help in some way...but you know."

Several times Chase's commanding officer invited our family over for BBQ; it was such a welcome reprieve. We were grateful that our children's friends' parents did not make them social outcasts like their parents.

On one hand, I wanted the days to go slower and for the clock to stand still, at least for now we were together until the trial. For now my Chase is safe on base.

On the other hand—when would we be able, if ever, to get on with our lives?

I was missing our friends back home more and more. If only Sara Nell, my dearest friend in Florida, were here to talk with. I had lost track of her. Sara Nell and her family had moved to another state at the same time we moved to Turkey and I did not have an address let alone a telephone number for them. Even if I could call her, I would not be able to talk candidly. I yearned to hear her loving voice with her charming southern accent say, "Hi, darlin'."

Chase and I both longed to be out of Turkey. At the same time, we were truly thankful that God had put such wonderful Turkish and American friends into our lives. We did miss the time spent with our dear Turkish friends and our loving Landlord and his wife.

Holidays

Thanksgiving had a new meaning this year for us all. We were very grateful that we were all together. The children got busy coloring turkey placemats for the big feast. Chase borrowed a friend's Webber smoker so he could smoke our turkey with applewood.

Chase and CJ got busy and made the stuffing to bake in the oven since they were roasting the turkey in the smoker.

Mia, Imp and Mom made pies. The girls insisted on each of us making our own. It took a little longer with an almost three-year-old trying to roll out the dough for her personal pie. (Mom made the filling). Imp's pie turned out to be quite unique.

It was a trick trying to convince Imp that she also had to participate in the clean-up.

Christmas

This day was one of the hardest holidays we had ever experienced. I had ordered presents for the children months ahead in case we were still in Turkey. We had been a little frugal on what we purchased because if we had returned to the States we would never have seen my orders and the money would be wasted.

There were a racecar track and cars for CJ, dolls and dress up clothes for Mia and a dollhouse for Imp.

Secretly, Chase and I were itching to play with the racecars when the owners were in bed.

Christmas trees were hard to come by. The base BX did try to bring in enough for every household. The trees were very straggly looking but with a few ornaments and some tinsel, we made it passable. Santa upon inspection would approve.

Christmas morning, as we watched the children open their gifts, we both choked back our tears.

Christmas with Everybody Home!

Neither one of us spoke the words aloud...that this could very well be our last Christmas together. Chase and I were having a difficult time being very joyous this day.

No More Easter Bunny

The next event turned out to be the Easter that Mia found out that there really was no Easter Bunny.

The Easter Bunny had gotten large stuffed rabbits for the girls and other gifts for CJ. The Easter Bunny then left the boxes in our little shed to be disposed of later.

Mia happened to go into the shed and find the packages addressed to me. She came directly to us and demanded an explanation of what this meant. We had to tell the truth...Mia was crushed.

Subsequently, she shared the news with her brother. He, however, was not quite sure if he believed her or not.

Mia and CJ's newfound knowledge caused a chain reaction. Now there was much concern and suspicion about Santa's existence as well.

They made the decision that they would choose to continue to believe in Santa. They did not think it was wise to question Santa's existence because there was, after all, too much at stake.

We heard CJ say to Mia, "If we don't believe in Santa, we may not get any more presents. I vote for Santa." Mia nodded her head in agreement.

This newfound information subsequently brought up suspicion about the Tooth Fairy. It was purely a snowball effect...to say the least.

Mia and CJ, 'being older and wiser,' decided to protect their little sister, now three-years-old, from this shocking information. They decided they must, at all costs, allow, her to continue with her child-like beliefs. They had become old sages.

Chapter 15
The Day of the Trial

10 Days Until C D 3

Our nerves were becoming quite frayed. It was now only ten days until C D 3. It was all we could do to stay composed—to assure the children and each other that everything was going to be okay.

Both Chase and I wanted to be strong and supportive of each other but at the same time, I think that Chase felt strangely overburdened from having that responsibility to bear.

The children still had no idea how serious the charges were. They only knew that Dad had to go back to court for something...once again.

Chase grew even more distant from us as the court date drew near. I am sure this was an effort to prepare himself mentally if things did not go well. On the other hand, I wanted to take advantage of each precious moment we had together. Moments we might not ever have again.

I wanted desperately to be close emotionally to Chase. I needed to feel our *oneness*...Chase needed to back off.

The Backup Plan

For the first time in months, the clothesline held a note from our Turkish friend.

The message read, "Dear friend: Please to come and meeting me in the same place. This matter is of importance much. Please be meeting at, 11 in morning tomorrow, if possible. If no, I shall wait upon arrival of you."

Having not been off the base since the last court date, I was, on one hand, looking forward to finally being able to step foot off this airplane patch...if even for just an hour. On the other hand, the base meant security and I was admittedly leery about leaving.

Each time I stepped off base there was a remote chance that I could be arrested for whatever reason. We knew the Turks did not need a valid excuse.

This meeting must be important or our Turkish friend would not be asking me to go off base. Chase and I agreed that I must go! The question now was how could I get past the guard at the front gate of the base?

I parked the car close to the checkpoint and held my breath as I walked past the guard. He nodded politely as I passed and told me to "be careful." Little did he know that I was so relieved that he did not stop me that I could have kissed him!

I walked the short distance to the village, as usual, dressed in an unassuming manner as possible and put a scarf on as soon as I was near the village.

Our friend was already there. He wanted Chase and me to consider a backup plan just in case—in case the verdict from the judge turned out to be a conviction.

Our friend said that the atmosphere with the Turkish/American tug-of-war in the Cyprus situation seemed to have improved some over the last few months. He was encouraged!

He felt that certain factions seemed to point toward a less Anti-American role by the Turkish officials. He wanted us to be aware that even if the Turkish Officials decided to set Chase free, there was still the problem of their "saving face."

I asked our friend, "How, then, do the Turks let Chase go and save face? Would this not be as good as admitting that this was all a trumped-up hoax?"

He responded, "Chase and the others are still very usable by the Turkish government."

Our friend's words were not very comforting and his next subject was even more unsettling. He said we definitely needed to consider a Plan B in case Chase should be imprisoned again...or... *I knew what 'or' meant!*

I listened carefully as he told me his plan—of the arrangements for Chase, the children and me to escape to Lebanon should things go badly for Chase.

For Chase, the plan was as follows: the guards on duty at the prison the first day or night of Chase's new imprisonment would have their backs turned when he escaped.

Chase would be met outside the prison and eventually be reunited with the children and me in Lebanon. Chase would not be traveling the same route as the children and me in case he was caught! He told me that it might be some length of time before they could get Chase safely to meet us!

Our friend asked if Chase suffered from seasickness! I said, "No." He then asked if Chase was a reasonable swimmer! I could only assume they might have an escape route for him by sea!

The children and I were to meet someone in the village just outside the base. I was to go there as soon I could get back to the base and gather the children after the trial was over.

We were to wait until as close to dark as feasible. We were not to take our car off base nor be carrying any belongings. It was to look as if we were going for a little stroll to the village to shop.

The children and I would be taken across Syria and into Lebanon. We would be in Beirut in a couple of weeks, if all went as planned. I was not told by what means we would be traveling or what route we would be taking. "It is better if you don't know," he said.

He assured me that we would be well cared for in Lebanon; our friend had friends in Beirut. We were told that Beirut, at least by Middle East standards, was a beautiful modern, safe city—at least at the present time.

He said there were good English schools that the children could attend and Chase's medical experience could be put to good use. He said he knew we would adapt well to that environment and we would be made to feel most welcome.

There was a house owned by his friend that would accommodate our family and it was available to us for as long as we needed to live there. He said it was not a large house but it had a small flower garden and it would be "okay by the American eye." It briefly ran through my mind that I might need to clarify if his, *okay,* was the same as our, *okay.*

This alternative plan was actually not the first time this idea had been mentioned to us. Subsequently, after the first thought of a Plan B, I had done some "what if'" legal investigation.

If we were to slip into another country, it would not be a

case of heading on back home to the good old U.S. of A. If Chase did return to the U.S., the Government must legally return him to Turkey because he was a military man.

I wondered, "Would the U.S. really send him back? Could we ever take that chance if we had to run?"

This would mean that if we were forced to use Plan B to save Chase's life the children and I could not return to the U.S unless we were to abandon Chase.

At best, we would only have a few more years before our passports ran out. I could not bear the thought of us not ever being able to return home—never to set foot on American soil.

This was not a decision to be made lightly especially for the children's sake. Was I/we again to be confronted with having to choose between our marriage, the children's future, our heritage as American citizens and Chase's career?

"Dear God, we need your help!"

Our friend was clear to point out that if we were forced to take the Plan B route it must be done simultaneously and without hesitation. We were not to tell anyone of this backup plan in advance—absolutely no one.

If the Turkish or American authorities were to realize that the children and I were gone, they would immediately be on guard. If Chase were to escape while we were still in the country, we would not be allowed to leave until he was found.

That night Chase and I discussed our friend's offer. We were somewhat relieved at having a Plan B. But, the price for all of us to pay would be so high!

A few days later, we left the answer to our friend in the clothesline. It read, "Dear Friend, We accept the offer of your hospitality. Thank you." As always, I was careful with what I wrote in my notes in case the wrong people intercepted them.

Our friend, in turn, had always written his notes using bad grammar so if the notes were intercepted it would be thought the note had been written by a common Turk. It was rather cute since our friend was very well educated.

Power of Attorney

In the meantime, Chase and I made out Powers of Attorney, *which* gave Steve authority to handle business transactions. If there were a need for him and his parents to take care of the children in the future, they would have what they legally needed. Sam was kind enough to notarize the papers for us.

I mentioned to Sam that I was worried about trying to mail these papers from the base. I hoped that we were not raising suspicion by sending these papers if, in fact, our mail was still being monitored. Sam then suggested that he make out an official-looking envelope that would go directly from his office to Steve. This way no one would realize the papers were coming from us.

While Sam made up the envelope, I wrote a quick note to Steve telling him these papers were for an emergency. Of course, I dare not mention Plan B.

We would need Steve to liquidate our assets if we had to use our backup plan and he could do nothing without these papers. The papers had to get to him straight on!

The Day of the Trial

Today was the day that would determine the direction of the balance of our lives and perhaps my beloved Chase's death sentence!

"I only wanted to lie in bed a few more minutes and cherish the comforting sound of Chase in the shower and the knowledge that the children were still happily snuggled down—safe in their beds."

I wondered if we would all be back here to sleep tonight, secure, or would we be running somewhere in the dark? This might be the last time I had a chance to look at our wedding book or the children's precious baby pictures. By tomorrow, we could have no possessions to hold or pass down to future generations.

If only I could make the clock stand still.

Oh, please! Do not let me start to cry out loud today. For if I do, I might never be able to stop.

One learns to cry on the inside, not the outside. We all have bravery inside; we simply must reach deep down and pull it up.

In life, each day, with each positive mark we make on that precious allotted time, we individually can become brave heroes.

Today, I have to summon up all the brave within me for Chase and the children and for myself.

I could not let the Turks see weakness...They will see what an American woman was made of.

I am, after all, my mother's bullheaded daughter.

The Chapel

Chase and I took the children to school and then we stopped by the base chapel. We held hands as we asked for *help* to get us through this day and to give us freedom.

As the sunlight streamed through the window, I asked the angels to fill the courtroom with their light and protection.

On our way to court, I had a million thoughts racing through my mind. Among them were, "What few things would be best for us to take...if we had to use Plan B."

We would have to leave almost all our possessions. I would dress us all in as many clothes as we could possibly get on and fill a large handbag with our most important papers. I tried to make a mental list: our college graduation rings, and the girl's first necklaces. I would need to go get all the cash I could and put it in a bag with the important papers.

I had to remember everything on my list if we had to run! But the one thing for sure I would not leave without was Imp's blankie!

The Courtroom

As we entered the courtroom, I was surprised to see it was almost devoid of both Turkish and American people.

I wondered, "Why was the room not crowded with hissing Turks as it was before? Was this a good sign or a bad one? Had this trial been put off again?"

Chase, Mack, and the Turkish lawyer went into the small room down the hallway to talk for a while.

I was told to "Have a seat." I felt somewhat put off, left out and annoyed. Besides, I felt very vulnerable sitting alone in that big old ominous room.

Knowing that at least we had Plan B, knowing that these last few minutes together with Chase would hopefully not be our last, was some consolation.

Would Plan B really work? I tried to shove the thought to the back of my mind that...anything could happen in this country, at any moment.

Soon, a few Turkish people came in and sat in the aisle

across from me. Then, a couple more came and sat in the back. These men were not of the common Turkish class; they were quite well dressed.

No one uttered a word. They sat and waited. A silent sense of foreboding seemed to be hovering in the room. It permeated the air. It was surreal!

The room was intolerably hot and I was feeling slightly sick to my stomach. At least there was not that awful smell in the room like there had been the time before.

The little cockroaches were still playing their same little games as Chase, Mack and the Turkish lawyer appeared.

Chase came over to me to talk for just a minute. He said the lawyers did not have much to say to him about what was going to transpire nor did they have any idea how long this fiasco would last.

They were trying to prepare him for the worst, he said. The Turkish lawyer told Chase he did not have a feeling for how the Turkish government had instructed the judge to rule!

Chase got up and went over to sit with his Turkish lawyer and Mack.

As we sat there, a few more Turkish men came in and soon two Americans entered just before the judge appeared.

The 'Trial' Got Under Way

Six armed military guards appeared and flanked Chase, distancing him from his Turkish lawyer and from Mack.

I had to choke down the fear inside. I had thought that I had prepared myself to handle this again, but I was wrong. Things had seemed so quiet until this moment.

Two more guards placed themselves at both ends of the row where I was sitting. I was glad that I was almost in the middle because it put distance between them and me.

Two more guards placed themselves as if for backup on the row where Mack and the Turkish lawyer were now sitting.

I felt that something strange was happening but I did not know what. All sorts of thoughts were swirling through my mind—Did this mean that Chase was about to be convicted of the charges? Could it mean they had found out about our Plan B?

They certainly were not there to offer Chase or me protection...so why this show of force right now?

The judge appeared. It was the same judge we had had the last two court dates. The judge motioned the Turkish lawyer to come forward with Chase. They did. So did the entire entourage of guards.

The judge naturally spoke in Turkish...this time very softly. Mack, Chase and I had no idea what he was saying. The decision about Chase's fate/our fate had obviously been made before we walked into this court.

There were no witnesses called. There were no statements or testimony, no rebuttal...nothing. Only the verdict!

Unexpectedly, the guards jerked up Chase, his Turkish lawyer, Mack, and me. We were taken to that small room. The guards remained outside with their guns in hand.

I was certain they had found out about our Plan B...but how?

Chase's Turkish lawyer had us sit down as he told the three of us the verdict: Chase had been found guilty and the sentence was life in prison!

I think that all the blood drained out of my head. It was all I could do to stand up and try to put my arms around Chase's neck. Chase held on tight to me—neither wanted to let go!

We could not feel. We could not think. We could not even cry! It was as if we were not in our body or even in the room!

It was impossible to process the news we had just received! It was unfathomable to think about the consequences of the Turkish Government verdict!

As we fought to bring our body and mind back to some state of functionality, the Turkish lawyer had something else to tell us.

He told us that the guilty sentence had been a two-part component!

First, the Sentence of Guilty did indeed carry a life sentence—if Chase behaved. If not, they could choose to change it to death at the will of the Turkish Government!

However, the Turkish authorities had decided that Chase's sentence of life in prison could be set-aside for the present time. The thought racing through my mind was, "*What the hell do they mean by present time?*"

Secondly, the lawyer said Chase's sentence would be placed in a probationary state. The lawyer explained that, in this case, probationary state meant that Chase was free to go and live his life, as long as he did not do this crime again or displease the Turkish Government in some way!

The Turks could decide to have him complete his sentence at any time they chose. Chase was free to choose to live in Turkey or leave the country and return to the U.S. to live while on this probation.

This was the Turkish way of saving face—of not admitting what the agenda had really been.

The judge had also told the Turkish lawyer that he and others had "Admiration for Chase and me and the children." The judge said, "We had the heart of Turks...not Americans."

I guess in his view that was a compliment. The judge also gave a bit of advice to the lawyer. The judge told him that, "Chase and his family should not be too quick to leave the country, for all concerned".

We could only assume he meant that it might somehow affect the other two men's fates. The judge made this point very clear. It was, of course, as clear as mud to us.

The Turkish lawyer wished us luck and told us to wait a few minutes while he took care of the formalities and then he left the room.

Chase, Mack, and I could not sit down; we just stood there fidgeting nervously! Some thirty minutes later, we were told that we could leave.

Who Played the Biggest Role

We will never really know who played the biggest role in the outcome of our circumstances.

Was it our Turkish friends?

Was it the pressure put on our Government by Ed Gurney and General Lemay?

Was it the lessening of steam in the pressure-cooker called Cyprus?

I Finally Collapsed

Our first instinct was to leave the courthouse, drive

back to the base, pack the suitcases and leave as soon as possible but that was not to be for many reasons.

Outside the courthouse, the base vehicle we had come in was waiting for us. Mack got in the front seat while Chase and I got in the back. It was close, clammy and miserably hot in the car. I found it hard to concentrate.

All of a sudden, there was a sharp pain on my left side. It felt like there was a weight placed on my chest I could hardly take a breath!

I passed out.

As I came back to consciousness, I heard Chase saying "That's all I need right now" meaning something to be wrong with me.

It would be an understatement to say that I felt betrayed and deeply hurt by the annoyed tone in his voice.

We went straight to the base hospital. I felt better by the time we drove through the gate. The doctor checked me out and did an EKG. I was OK.

The pressures of this year had finally caught up with me all at once. The Doc said that stress would do that and instructed me to go home and relax.

Chase wanted to go back to our trailer to get the car to drive me home but I felt good enough to walk the few blocks from the hospital to our quarters.

As soon as we got in the door, he hugged me and apologized for his response when I had passed out. I tried to understand—he, too, had had about all he could handle at that moment...but his response definitely caught me off guard.

After all the hell I had gone through, too, I was not expecting that reaction from my Chase again!

We had a few hours before the children were to get out

of school and we took advantage of the time. We needed to unwind. We snuggled on the couch and took an hour's nap.

The Phone Rang

Our nap was interrupted by the phone ringing. It was Chase's Commander calling with his congratulations. He told Chase to take the next two days off for leave... *Whoop di doo!*

Chase's Commanding Officer said *They* wanted Chase in *the office* at ten o'clock in the morning for a debriefing.

The children were unbelievably happy about it all being over. They decided it was cause for their usual go-to treat, Ho Hos and coffee for dessert.

They were, however, unhappy about the prospect of moving only a few weeks before school was out for the year.

Chase and I had so prepared ourselves for the worst that we were having difficulty adjusting to the nightmare almost being over...especially Chase.

We would still have a little while to wonder if we really were going to be allowed to leave. There was always the possibility that the Turks could, at any moment, change their minds and drag Chase/us back into hell!

Chase was anxious to hear what they had to say at the meeting the following morning. We wondered what our next step would be.

At the meeting, Chase was told that even if the Turkish government would, in the future, request his return to Turkey that it would probably not happen.

The remainder of the meeting was centered around where we would be based; when and how we would get there; and about the future of his military career.

It was made *crystal clear* to Chase that his continued career with the Air Force would be contingent on his/our silence concerning this incident in Turkey.

We were never to say a word about our ordeal—about the hell we had been through!

Ten Long Days

Ten long days went by before we would receive Chase's orders...to Germany!

"Why Germany?" We asked ourselves, "Were they trying to keep us away from the American press?" As if we were interested in dragging this ordeal out any longer! We wondered if they really thought we wanted to verbalize it repeatedly to strangers or if we wanted to jeopardize Chase's career?

Even though I still had many of our belongings in boxes, it would take time to pack and go through the normal base processing to leave.

We lived each day with trepidation—counting the days and hours until we would be truly free from all of this.

Chapter 16
A Few Hours to Freedom

One Week Out and Trouble Ahead

Then a note in the clothesline appeared one-day from our Turkish friends!

It read, *"Please dear friends to stay safely within in your American base. There are more troubles concerning Cyprus problem. Be cautious there may be possibility for someone to try to punish Chase further by arresting or injuring wife. May Allah protect you!"*

"Were we this close to freedom, only to be pulled back into this nightmare once again?" We were only ten days away from getting out of this hell!

Chase got a call shortly after we got the note. He was to report to his Commander's office. His Commander said he felt that we must all leave as soon as possible.

The first available civilian flight out of Turkey was some fifty-two hours from then.

When the children got home from school, we told them we were going to have to leave a little earlier. They would only miss about a week of school and they could say goodbye to their friends in the morning.

It was good that by now we only had the suitcases left

to pack. The household goods were already on their way to Germany.

The next morning I went to school, explained the situation to the teacher and she had the children's records ready by lunchtime. The children said their tearful goodbyes to their friends before we returned home to finish packing our remaining stuff.

Chase was busy at the same time doing all that he had to do to clear the base. He had to get his orders to travel, base clearance, our airplane tickets, and such.

Chase was informed that now, instead of Germany, we were going back to the States.

But, but, but, our furniture and car were on their way to Germany!

A Few More Hours

We were finally leaving in a few hours.

It was alarming that we were not flying on a U.S. Air Force plane and we would take off from a runway on this base.

"If only we did not have to leave from a Turkish-controlled airport."

The fighters on the flight line and one U-2 spy plane here on this base were certainly no transportation for a family. There was no other appropriate aircraft nearby. Supposedly, there were no Air Force Air EVAC planes that could be made available any sooner either.

Chase was extremely frustrated and so was I.

Once we left the relative safety of the base, we could be at risk. We would be vulnerable not only here in Adana's Airport but also when we changed planes in Ankara.

They/He either did not quite understand the jeopardy this could place us in or did not care. Perhaps this was *His* last chance to give us grief.

Chase tried to get through to one of his friends who was a Commander of a squadron in Italy. He had long-range planes under his command. Perhaps he could help find transportation directly from this base. Chase knew his friend had the authority to deploy a plane to pick us up!

Chase called his friend's office but, as luck would have it, his friend was on leave back to the States for two weeks.

Oddly, after Chase's call to his friend in Italy our telephone went dead. We were still being monitored!

"How rude. They had not even left us a staticky dial tone!"

Time to Leave the Base

I had dreamed of this day but I had not envisioned the apprehension of what might be around each corner or who might be waiting for us at either airport.

"*Now, Sondra*," I told myself, "*Do not let your mind make this worse.*"

When we left the base, we were driven out of a side gate and into town via side roads, trying to avoid any crowds. In order to get out to the airport, we finally had to travel on one of the main streets. There were anti-American signs on several stores as we drove past. Now we understood the need to get us out of Turkey so quickly.

Sadly, our route took us past our Turkish friend's home. The children wanted to stop and say goodbye to their friends in our old neighborhood but we dare not. Nor could we let them stop and buy their favorite Turkish bread. We felt bad that we could not grant them their small requests.

The children, again, had no idea why we were leaving early. They did not know the apprehension we had at that very moment. Chase and I tried to act as nonchalant as possible but it was not easy.

As the car bounced along, my thoughts drifted back to that first night we arrived...of the sights and sounds of this mysterious land and of the innocence we had.

The Airport

The car drove up to the airport. We felt "so far so good."

Relief...everything seemed normal. Mercifully, there were no police or military vehicles anywhere in our line of sight.

As we stepped inside the terminal, we saw only two armed police standing near the door that led out to the runway where the small plane was parked. We were not particularly alarmed by their presence.

Chase handed the agent our tickets and soon we were ready to board the plane. There were about a dozen other passengers in line ahead of us.

Imp was walking beside me as we went through the door. All of a sudden, one of the policemen grabbed her! He pulled her hand out of mine and started running with her in his arms!

He ran toward a police car that was sitting in full sight!

I cannot begin to explain the panic that Chase and I felt! We started to run after him. Then, the policeman stopped, turned around and started laughing hilariously.

He was playing with her. He was pretending that he was going to steal her "because she was such a beautiful, blond *Bebeck*" (baby).

It took Chase and me a minute or so to gain our composure. We tried to smile and act as if he had just played a funny joke on us.

That policeman would never know that he had just taken ten years off our lives!

The others passengers had boarded the plane and were all seated. There were enough seats for the five of us but not altogether. As would be expected, the passengers were all Turkish except for us.

After we were seated, all in separate seats, except for Imp and me, Chase motioned to me from across the aisle to look out the window.

There they were—three Turkish military vehicles with several men in each. They all got out with rifles in their hands. They all turned toward the plane. They took a few steps forward and stopped, then put their rifles to rest at their side.

They knew we were on that plane. They wanted us to know they knew. It was a game of cat and mouse.

More questions ran through my mind: Did this then mean that someone would be waiting for us when we landed in Ankara? Were we really going to be allowed to leave the country? Were they just waiting to get us away from the protection of the base before they pounced again?

The pilot revved up the motors and immediately we were taxiing down the bumpy, old tarmac strip. The plane jerked and rumbled into the air.

We were safe for now!

A Welcome Diversion

We were provided with both food and entertainment on the flight to Ankara. As they did on the flight into Adana when we arrived so long, long ago, the stewardess gave us an orange and a bottle of water. By now, it was very welcome as Chase and I had not eaten all day. The children were not hungry or thirsty because we had fed them before we left the base.

The stewardess came back and asked us if we would permit her to show the children the cockpit—naturally, we said, '"Yes."

Now, mind you, we could all see everything the pilot was doing, as the plane was very small. The pilot invited CJ to be the first. The pilot let CJ sit on his lap and showed him how to fly the plane. CJ was delighted. He got about a ten-minute flying lesson.

Next was Mia. She was instructed in the same manner and for approximately the same amount of time. Mia was equally as pleased. Mia did mention the pilot "had funny breath"...only from a child.

Then, it was Imp's turn. Since Imp was only three, we are a bit apprehensive, but we were okay.

The pilot was totally enchanted with this cute round-faced blond nymphet. He could not resist granting this child her every wish.

Unfortunately, her wish was to drive herself without any help from him. He had no qualms about granting our nymphet's wish. The plane flew reasonably level for at least about thirty seconds before it veered first to one side and then to the other, tossing water and oranges everywhere.

I do not know who was enjoying this experience more—the nymphet or the pilot. There seemed no end to the fun these two were having and there seemed no end to the havoc these two were creating behind them.

We heard someone say something about "killing that child" (that was not exactly the words they were using). I was ready to second the motion when I remembered the nymphet was ours.

Chase, being the brave man he was, worked his way up to the cockpit and saved us all. He removed the unwilling nymphet from the cockpit. The pilot was most displeased with Chase for taking his entertainment away.

The other passengers, with full right, glared at us for the rest of the flight to Ankara.

Ankara

We were only to have forty-five minutes between the time we landed in Ankara and we were to board the next plane.

Our itinerary took us first to London with two stops in between and then on to New York City.

The fewer minutes we had on the ground in Ankara, the less vulnerable we would be!

Hopefully, this would be our last Turkish hurdle to jump!

My mind was racing, "Would we actually be allowed to board our final flight? Is this where they arrest Chase again? And, if they do arrest Chase again, what can I do now in an unfamiliar city, knowing no one, with three children and a plane to board in only a few minutes?"

The buildings of Ankara came into view on the horizon and soon we were descending. I feared what or who would be waiting on the ground for us.

The sight of the Turkish soldiers standing there, sending us a message at the airport in Adana when we left, was still etched into our minds.

The plane bounced onto the runway and came to a screeching stop in front of a real airport terminal. The pilot said his last goodbyes to his little Buddy Imp as we left the plane. The nymphet, of course, wanted to drive some more.

We found our luggage and dragged it to the building.

There were fewer people than we were hoping for in the terminal. We wanted to be able to get lost in the crowd.

As we checked in our last bag and were handed the boarding passes, we saw a man at the ticket counter motioning to another man and pointing our way!

Our adrenalin started to pump as the two military guards came toward us! Our concern grew when we turned around and saw at least a dozen guards scattered throughout the terminal.

It was obvious we were the focus of their attention!

Our instinct was to run but we did not dare—not with the children. Besides, running could be exactly what they were trying to force us into...yet another incident!

"Now I know I had been in this country too long and was beginning to think like a Turk."

Chase and I simultaneously looked at each other; we knew our course. We had to be calm. We had to pretend they did not exist... *These bastards could not make us wet our pants.*

We were, all but personally escorted to the plane by the armed military guards. At least it was toward the plane and not out of the terminal to who knows where, or what!

The military guard's demeanor was daunting. Were they there to send us a message or were they just waiting for us to slip up?

Is Chase or I about to be arrested or shot or are we truly on our way to freedom...to home?

Chase told me to take the children so he could put distance between him and us in case they started to shoot!

He told me to board the plane with the children no matter what happened to him.

Reluctantly, I kept walking with Mia and CJ in front of me and Imp in my arms as Chase followed a distance behind!

I could not fathom that the Turks would shoot at Chase when he was so close to the plane! Then again, they were standing to the side of us and they would have a clear shot.

Shivers ran up my back as I braced myself for, perhaps, that sickening sound of a gun going off behind us!

As we walked toward the plane, seconds seemed like minutes, but, miraculously, no shot rang out!

Aboard at Last

Soon, we heard the welcome creek of the steel steps under our feet and the stewardess welcoming us as we walked through the door of the plane.

With our minds in a fog, we found our seats and buckled in the children and ourselves.

Next, the firm thud of the bulkhead door closing and the door handle being secured was more than music to our ears.

Then the sense for at least this moment we were locked in safe and sound.

I kept repeating in my head, *"Please God, let this be real and not a dream!"*

Each sequence of events toward the preparation for departure became one more step toward freedom. We hardly dared to breathe!

My mind had only one focus—to get this plane off the ground before someone changed their mind...*I wish I knew how to levitate.*

The stairs were pushed away from the plane. At last, the engines started to whine. Two more steps toward freedom.

The passenger on the side of the plane next to the terminal speculated about the presence of all the armed Turkish soldiers flanking the plane. One man sitting directly behind me assured his wife, "There must be some Turkish VIP aboard this flight."

Little did he realize that sitting immediately in front of him and his wife was a family whose lives were hanging in the balance!

The plane began to move and then taxi away from the terminal. Our hearts raced from fright that our plane would come to a screeching halt. We were afraid that some Turkish official might give the orders to stop us from our journey.

In the time it takes to process the reality that we were soon to be to safety, the plane lurched forward. The runway soon swallowed up as the plane rumbled down the tarmac.

With an upward jerk, the wheels of the plane lifted off the ground and pulled the five of us up toward heaven, past the soldiers, beyond our fear.

The gentle thud of the wheels being locked back into the plane's wheel-well seemed to be our final affirmation that there would be no turning back.

The wings of the plane tip slowly as we change course for our next stop, Italy.

Crimson Sun

As we came slowly about, laid out before us for the last time was the contrasting picture of the beautiful, foreboding, mysterious sights of Ankara.

There it was, the crimson sun, sinking down between the tall, slender, minarets of the mosques. It was soon to cast its shadows on this land of heaven and hell!

It was hard to assimilate that this scene laid out before us was almost identical to the sights we saw the night we arrived now almost two, long years ago.

Strange, I could still feel the excitement of the night we arrived in Adana, the expectations of new adventures yet to be unfolded, and the excitement of naive explorers!

A Bitter Sweet Farewell

My mind drifted back to Turkey. My heart felt so full with love and gratitude for our dear, dear Turkish friends. Quietly in my mind, I send them my love and eternal gratitude! ♥

CJ, Mia and I were sitting on the left side of the plane while Chase and Imp sat across from us.

Chase leaned over and kissed Imp's head and then, looking across the aisle, he blew me a kiss then winked his special wink.

I could see Chase swallowing hard, trying to hold back

all the emotions that he too was feeling!

Thank you, God, we did not have to use Plan B!

Thank you, God, Chase is flying home with me!

I, unlike Chase, could no longer hold back the tears. The tears of joy and relief filled my eyes and started pouring down my face.

CJ unbuckled his seatbelt, pushed past his sister, sat on my lap and cupped my face with both his little hands as he said, "Mommy, it's okay to cry. You're a very good girl."

Then, Mia who was sitting next to me, slipped her little hand in mine and said, "Mommy, are we really okay?"

I responded, "Yes, my darlings, mommy's tears are happy tears. We're just fine!"

When our ordeal was over and we were allowed to return to the U.S., my husband remained in the service until his retirement. He was reminded that his continued career in the service and any promotions would be dependent on his/our silence concerning this incident.

Chase now rests in Arlington cemetery. This story can now be told!

The Reason for Sharing this Story is Two-fold

First, to confirm to every woman, both young and old, that we are strong and we have Brave deep down inside— All we have to do is reach down and pull it up.

This story is not meant in any way, to discount the bravery of my Chase. He too had to reach down and pull up his Brave.

It is said that there are two sides to every story. I have chosen to share in full the usually overlooked, other side, of many stories.

This story is dedicated to every military and responder's wife who reaches down and pulls her Brave up every day. To each woman around the world who does the same, no matter what her circumstance!

Secondly, it is both ironic and sad that more than fifty years later that our story is as likely to happen to someone else today as it did to us years ago in the Middle East.

The dates have changed but the circumstances remain almost the same.

Never To Be Forgotten

I believe that God placed exactly the right people, both American and Turkish, at exactly the right time in our lives. Who knows what the outcome would have been had this not been so!

Our *dear Turkish friends* whose names will have to remain unknown for their safety—We love you and are eternally grateful!

Sam and Mary and 'Legal Eagle' Mack who stood by us—We have *no* words to express our *appreciation* for your help!

Steve Demopoulos, Congressman Ed Gurney, and General Curtis Lemay—You were our knights in shining armor! We hope to join you in Heaven someday!

Our wonderful children Mia, CJ, and Imp, who endured this trek with us—Thank you for being you!

To: Chase, my husband, now deceased, *"we made it through, my love, though not unscathed."*

Made in the USA
San Bernardino, CA
01 May 2019